How Did They Get Taller Than Me?

Kathy Woodbury

ISBN 978-1-64559-555-7 (Paperback)
ISBN 978-1-64559-556-4 (Digital)

Covenant Books, Inc.
11661 Hwy 707
Murrells Inlet, SC 29576
www.covenantbooks.com

Jesus continued, "There was a man who had two sons."

—Luke 15:11

Be shepherds of God's flock that is under
your care, watching over them—

—1 Peter 5:2a

Contents

Preface

Just Obey

Trying to get my son to do what I asked, I finally implored him to JUST OBEY! Stopping to think, he announced a truth that emanated from his childlike wisdom. "Mama, obeying is just not that easy all the time." He was right. I love to write, but I struggled with the thought that God may be asking me to write a book. I began writing in journals in college and have continued over the years. I write what God says to me, what I feel, and what I am going through; and often, I write my prayers. I don't punctuate correctly, or write in complete sentences, nor do I write every day; but I write. When the boys were born, I started writing down what they said and what they did. I began this adventure by writing on a baby calendar every day, and then I wrote in their baby books. I crossed over to cute little journals, but as they became more active, I wrote on bits and pieces of paper or anything I could get my hands on at the time. When we came on active duty in the military and our many traveling adventures began, I started doing something I said I would NEVER do—write Christmas letters! I couldn't help myself, so I wrote them each year, and it helped me chronicle our lives as well as the growth of our boys. From those writings, several people suggested I write a book. I laughed it off and took those suggestions as sweet affirmations. But the thought continued to develop, and I could not let it go. I believe that for whatever reason, God has put it on my heart to write down my experiences and thoughts on raising children in a book. I committed. Although it took over twenty years to write, I decided to obey what I believe God asked of me. It didn't matter how long it took to complete the book, but only that I obeyed.

When I began my writing, I mentioned it to the boys. Matt, my youngest son, asked if I were going to name names. Oh yes, this is the kind of book where you name names. So to my boys, whose names are Ben and Matt, I thank you for allowing me to share our life experiences—good and bad. God has grown you both up, and he has taught me so much in the process. May this book be a gift to you as a written reminder of God's work in your lives. Prayerfully, your wives will treasure the process of growth written here that gave them the men they now have married. And maybe, my grandchildren can benefit from your growth as you allow God to teach you to grow your children to know Him and love Him first. Thank you. I love you!

To my mama and daddy, I thank you that as God entrusted me to you, you raised me to first know and love Him. Your faith, prayers, and encouragement have always been an anchor even when my worries attempted to derail God's purpose for me. Thank you. I love you!

To Mama Jane, I thank you for raising a son, my husband, to have a very tender heart toward God. You have included me in your life as your daughter, and I am blessed with your love and encouragement. Thank you. I love you!

To my husband, Greg, God gave you to me to be my most important treasure, my best friend, my most faithful partner in this great adventure of parenting. I love you forever and am most grateful for what a phenomenal husband and extraordinary daddy you are. Thank you. I love you!

Fear Not—I Present an Imperfect Family

"You are pregnant," the doctor announced.

But I went to the doctor because I thought I had the flu! Now Greg and I were staring at each other with no words but, "Wait, what?"

We had been married over five years at the time and had tried to have a child, but nothing. A doctor had even told Greg he would be unable to have children. Turned out that wasn't true and here we were! Of course, you can imagine our excitement as we told everybody we could find and then began to prepare for our new little family member.

Each month going to the doctor, seeing the baby grow, and fixing the nursery added to my elation. Until one day, I looked down at my HUGE belly and thought, "That big thing has to come OUT."

My excitement and elation then turned to FEAR. Adding to my fear was the cultural phenomena that happened the further along one got in pregnancy—every woman has a horror story of her delivery that she is determined to share. I soaked in this fear for a while, rehearsing the unknown in my mind. But what was unknown to me was totally known to God. He had created my body to give birth. He knew what He was doing, and I was going to trust Him and fear not.

So with my "you made my body" mantra, I completed my pregnancy with no fear of birth. Until one Sunday night in August, I stayed home from church because I was in terrible pain. Since it was my first child, I didn't know what to expect; and around midnight, I finally called the hospital to see if maybe I was beginning to have the baby. The nurse I spoke to in Sumter, South Carolina, drawled out these poignant words, "Honey, if you're talkin' rite now, then you aren't havin' a baby."

ARE YOU KIDDING ME? I WON'T BE ABLE TO TALK WHEN HAVING A BABY? Greg, being totally satisfied with the answer, directed me to get some sleep since I must just be anxious. He proceeded to the couch in the den while I stayed awake all night repeating to God, "You made my body." At my regularly scheduled doctor appointment the next day, he affirmed my work and announced that I would be having my baby that night. At this point, I was not afraid of how the baby would come out; I just wanted him OUT! I guess that was how God worked! That night, at around nine thirty, Benjamin Lloyd Woodbury was born.

No fear—until we got him home and the sobering realization sank in that we were now parents and had a real person to care for, teach, nurture and help grow; and we had NO EXPERIENCE! God was so smart to let us start easy with feeding, bathing, and diapering to build our confidence in parenting. To be honest though, off and on, I had fears mounting about how I would be as a parent. Would I do it right? I didn't want to do anything that would scar my son's life. And more than that, I wanted to help them become exactly what God had desired them to be when He thought of them. The pressure that I placed on myself created fear. As they grew, the tasks of parenting grew. It was no longer just feeding, clothing, and security; but it was molding a person who would grow, learn, and make decisions on their own.

Sometimes, I questioned my readiness and my ability to parent competently. The circumstances of being a military family with deployments and moves often added to my fears. My questions sometimes kept me up at night—questions that changed as they grew. Greg was deployed much of his first duty station when the boys were very young. I was concerned about them needing their daddy. Our moving every couple of years brought rise to questions about the boys changing schools constantly, participating in sports, connecting with good friends, and being a part of communities instead of just passing through. Would my boys have the same opportunity as other children? I grew up going to the same church all my life, having great opportunities for children's programs, youth groups, and camp opportunities. But the boys were always moving, always going to chapel where things were so different from the local church, and were never the same from one place to another. I worried that their spiritual growth would somehow be lacking. What about not getting to be with grandparents? They were the only kids on the team that didn't have family besides parents yelling from the stands. They missed out on most extended-family functions. Would they be close to extended family? The ultimate questions came down to wondering: how would my boys turn out? Would I do a good-enough job that they would be successful? Most importantly, would I do the right things to help them know and love Jesus first and with all their heart? Maybe you have never questioned your parenting or maybe you have never had fears that what you said or did through the circumstances of your child's life would be wrong, but I have!

My oldest son was ten years old, and before moving from Albuquerque, New Mexico to Guam, we took a month to visit family. I was so excited because my little skinny boy was filling out. His cheeks were getting so full and his legs somewhat pudgy. But the fullness in his body was not good, but very bad, and I didn't even know it! I didn't recognize it. He began to be very sick while at my mom's, so we eventually took him to the doctor. Tests showed his blood pressure was extremely high, and his kidneys were beginning to fail. As instructed, we rushed him to a pediatric nephrologist about an hour away where he was immediately admitted to the hospital. Nurse after nurse attempted to put an IV into his dehydrated little body. As the nurses worked furiously with tears in their eyes, Ben calmly encouraged them with, "It's okay. It's not your fault." Finally, someone from pediatric intensive care came and successfully inserted the IV.

Many tests were performed that day, and a kidney biopsy was scheduled for the next day. With our life, move, and mostly our little boy's health up in the air, we prayed. I was not in control. I didn't see it coming. I couldn't protect my little boy. For heaven's sake, I thought he was just getting chunky! What kind of a mom was I? Fears, feelings of inadequacy, and helplessness filled my heart as we waited for the doctor to call with the results of the last tests. Then the call came. The best call we had ever gotten. Although just the beginning of a long haul back to health, my son's blood results were getting better with the medication. For now, he would no longer need a kidney biopsy.

Slowly over the course of a year or so, Ben's blood pressure returned to normal, and his kidneys were not permanently harmed. He had a condition known as poststreptococcal glandular nephritis. It was an attack on his kidneys caused by an undetected strep infection. I didn't know anything about this illness. I remembered that a couple of weeks prior, during the packing of our house, Ben had a sore throat; but he slept it off, was better the next day, and never complained about it again. I suddenly felt another pang of incompetency in my parenting. Although ridiculously unfounded, I encountered a shame of not being able to recognize my child's illness. With total drama, but also with a hint of truthfulness, I declared, "I can't do this! I can't parent! I don't know enough!" As a mother of eight- and ten-year-old boys, it was a little late to be giving up. After all, they had made it this far. But they had made it this far with one important influence. The first night that Ben was in the hospital, when we were praying and awaiting test results, my husband was sitting by Ben's bed. I heard him quietly comfort Ben with these words, "Ben, I am your dad. I will watch over you all night. I will never leave your side." THAT'S IT! That's how I can parent! My God, my Heavenly Father, is with me every step of the way and will never leave me alone with this job. "But he said to me, 'My grace is sufficient for you, for my power is made perfect in weakness. Therefore, I will boast all the more gladly about my weaknesses, so that Christ's power may rest on me" (2 Corinthians 12:9).

My fears and doubts about my parenting stemmed from the very real understanding that I am flawed. I am not perfect. I didn't want my defects to hinder the boys' growth, their personality, or their becoming what God had for them. My fear never debilitated me nor caused me not to be an active mom. But I just sometimes had nagging concerns. As I parented and as the boys grew, I also grew. I learned to parent babies; then I learned to parent toddlers; then I learned to parent boys in elementary school, middle school, and high school; and I especially had much learning to do when they were in college. There were two things that I used in order to learn how to parent without fear: God's word and the fellowship of Christian women. I gleaned much hope from the Bible, claiming the verse that, "All your sons will be taught by the Lord, and great will be your children's peace" (Isa. 54:13) His word was a lamp to my feet and a light to my path. I had to learn what the verse in Colossians 3:16 meant when it said, "Let the word of Christ dwell in you richly as you teach and admonish one another with all wisdom, and as you sing psalms, hymns and spiritual songs with gratitude in your hearts to God." I can never overstate the power of fellowship with other moms in my life. From Protestant Women of the Chapel Bible studies, to my Moms in Touch groups, to ladies Bible study at the local church, I learned from women who had parented and from women who were parenting the same time I was. We experienced the drama, the fun, the questions, and hurts of parenting together. Somehow, in this shared life of raising children, the task became more manageable, more exciting, and more of a blessing. I still made many mistakes along the way; but God's grace, mercy, and patience with me as I parented alleviated my fears and concerns, and enabled me to parent boldly without fear. I was always able to say to the boys, "I am sorry. I messed up. Will you forgive me?" And they also were able to extend me grace. I found a scrap of paper from September 19, 2000, that I had written this experience. "Ben showed me grace today. I failed as a mom. I fussed badly. He came and asked me to lay down with him, and he held me so tight. He loved me when I didn't deserve it. He said he would always love me. Ben showed me grace today." I love what Oswald Chambers said in his book, *My Utmost for His Highest*, "Never let the sense of failure corrupt your new action."

When Ben was very young, he made the statement to me that he bet that God wanted him and Matt back with Him in heaven. I guess he figured that God missed them. Ben was right. God wants us to give our children back to Him and allow Him to grow them. God does not give us these children and say, "Okay, the rest is up to you." I accepted that I can't grow them; God can grow them, and I am going to let Him. Yes, I will let Him through me and in spite of me. I can still see his little arms stretching wide, his muscles tightening, and his fists bulging as Ben sang his favorite song. The intensity with which he delivered each line while stomping his feet with his high-top basketball shoes would make a believer out of the hardest soul. Loudly and without reservation, Ben spewed forth these words:

> "My God is so big, so strong, and so mighty.
> There's nothing my God cannot do (clap clap).
> My God is so big, so strong, and so mighty.
> There's nothing my God cannot do (clap clap).
> The mountains are His, the rivers are His, the stars are His handiwork too (clap clap).
> My God is so big, so strong, and so mighty.
> Yes, He can do all things through you" (clap clap).

When Ben sang, I joined in loudly and affirmed his excitement and his faith. Yes, He can do all things through you! When awake at night concerned about whether I was "doing it right," I remembered that in spite of my shortcomings in my parenting, regardless of the circumstances of our military family, God could and would work. "My God is so big, so strong, and so mighty." When I know the character of God, I can trust that He is able to more than atone for the weakness in my parenting, and to alleviate any concerns, questions, and fears. I only have to look at the words of Isaiah to be humbled at the bigness of God, "Who has held the dust of the earth in a basket, or weighted the mountains on the scales and the hills in a balance?" (Isa. 40:12). Many verses declare God's strength, and 1 Chronicles 16:11 encourages us to, "Look to the Lord and His strength, seek his face always." God will grow our children. I have to be faithful to water. I have to water often, consistently, with God's direction, and without fear.

Things always work out when we place them in God's hands. Ben started college wanting to play baseball. Neither he nor Matt ever wanted to go into the military, and after seeing the cadets while being stationed at the Air Force Academy, they were vehemently opposed. The kids at the college Ben first attended were so confused by his gypsy lifestyle that they soon told the others not to ask Ben where he was from because it took so long for him to explain. Later that first year of school, we broke the news to Ben that after college, or age twenty-three, he would no longer have a military identification card and would lose access to the bases. I'm not sure that this realization prompted the next action, but soon after that discovery, Ben put down his baseball, changed to a college with an ROTC program, and decided he wanted to try the military. When we asked him why, especially after his total rejection of the idea at first, he just stated, "I loved our life." He is currently a 1LT in the Army. He will probably not stay in the military for long though. Why? He has a wife and child, and he has learned that the Army lifestyle is slightly different from our Air Force one. He loves being with his little family. He chooses to be a family man. We couldn't ask for anything better as parents. The questions of raising my boys and raising them in the military were so real at the time. But God's presence, help, and work in our life were more real. I counted on the verse in Matthew 7, "If you, though you are evil, know how to give good gifts to your children, how much more will your Father in heaven give good gifts to those who ask him!" God loved my boys more than I could.

My boys are not perfect. They came from and were raised by imperfect parents. I could elaborate on our imperfections, but I'm sure you will read about some of them in the pages to follow. But the work of God in our life as a family is real. My boys know Jesus, and they desire to follow him. So why was I afraid of the task set before me as a mom? God gave us Ben and Matt, and God gave us every tool we needed to parent them. "Unless God builds the house, its builders labor in vain" (Ps. 127:1). I asked as Samson's parents, "Oh Lord, I beg you, let the man of God you sent to us come again to teach us how to bring up the boy who is to be born" (Judg. 13:8). God is our teacher. He promises, "I will instruct you and teach you in the way you should go. I will counsel you and watch over you" (Ps. 32:8). Parenting is hard, and parenting is sometimes scary. But God gave us about 365 verses in the Bible, instructing us not to be afraid—one for every glorious and not so glorious day of parenting! Do not be afraid because our competency is in Christ. "Not that we are competent in ourselves to claim anything for ourselves, but our competence is from God" (2 Cor. 3:5).

During our pregnancy, we went back to the doctor each month to get a report on how the baby was growing. Between doctor visits, I just ate and rested and ate and ate and went about my daily work. I didn't form the baby or make him grow. I just fed him. I did have the normal concerns about the baby being healthy, but I knew that the One who was "knitting the baby together in my womb" (Ps. 139:13) would be faithful to His task. Nine months later, and many, many pounds later, a perfect baby appeared! How did that happen? God! One morning, standing in church singing away, I suddenly felt dwarfed by two very tall young men on either side of me. Wait a minute, I'm the Mom, these are my little boys, and how did they get taller than me? All I did was feed them, feed them, and feed them. But I didn't cause them to grow. I don't even know when it happened. First Corinthians 3:6 says, "I planted the seed, Apollos watered, God made it grow." In the case, I guess my husband planted the seed, we watered, and God made them grow. Feed the word, and God grows them spiritually. Feed the love, and God grows them socially and emotionally. Feed the knowledge, and God grows them mentally. And feed the groceries, and well, God makes them taller than me!

I Want to Be...a Fighter Pilot?

From the front seat of the car, I listened as a heated debate developed behind me where my five- and three-year-old sons were sitting. Matt was sharing with his older brother that he was going to be a fighter pilot when he grew up, and Ben was firing back with the numerous problems he had identified with Matt's career choice. Totally frustrated, Ben finally asked me, "Mom, don't you have to be what Jesus wants you to be?" Not realizing I was being sucked into Ben's agenda, I affirmed his convictions. With all the ammunition and righteous authority he needed, Ben proceeded to instruct Matt, "Jesus does not want you to be a fighter pilot!" With that comment, the conversation was over. Matt is not a fighter pilot.

If only our vocational decisions were that easy. We may not all have an older brother who plays the Holy Spirit for us, but as believers, we all have the Holy Spirit to guide us to exactly what God has planned for us. When I was a little girl, I knew I wanted to be a preacher's wife. I have no idea why, nor did I pursue this—didn't just date "preacher boys." In college, I majored in fine arts just because I liked to draw, and I had waited until the last minute to declare a major. But I wasn't very competitive in the field. I double minored in business and religion, so I joked that I would open a religious art business.

Between my junior and senior year in college, much to my surprise, I was selected to be a Baptist Student Union Summer Missionary in New Orleans. After much prodding, I agreed to go. Why would God send an art major, who enjoyed working with youth in the local church, to the inner city to work in a Baptist center? Maybe it was because a three-year-old boy wandering around alone after midnight needed someone to give him a hotdog. Maybe it was because an old lady who lived by herself and never saw her children needed a young white girl to bring her leftover baked goods in a shopping cart, and sit and talk each week. Maybe it was because a group of hardened teenagers needed to be listened to and to see that someone would care for them. Maybe God wanted to show me that I was created to "do unto the least of these."

Psalm 139:13–17 says, "For you created my inmost being, you knit me together in my mother's womb. I praise you because I am fearfully and wonderfully made, your works are wonderful. I know that full well. My frame was not hidden from you when I was made in the secret place. When I was woven together in the depths of the earth, your eyes saw my unformed body. All the days ordained for me were written in your book, before one of them came to be. How precious to me are your thoughts. O God, How vast is the sum of them!" Knowing this, I decided that I wanted to be exactly what God intended for me to be when he thought of me before I was in my mother's womb. Wow! That was freedom. That meant I should be perfectly secure, perfectly satisfied, perfectly at peace because God's thoughts and plans for me are not wrong.

After the summer in New Orleans, I finished college and went to Seminary to earn my masters in church social work. In the meantime, I married my preacher. God is good. Some years later, I reflected on my status—I was a social worker with a job I loved, and I was a preacher's wife. But still, I wasn't complete. I knew what I wanted. Soon, I became Ben and Matt's mom! God had given me a high calling, and as the seasons of my life changed, what I wanted to be changed also. I was a social worker by trade, a preacher's wife by marriage, but a stay-at-home mom by calling and choice.

Great! End of story, right? Fulfillment and completion, right? Perfectly satisfied and perfectly at peace, right? As a mother of babies and toddlers, there were days in a row that I walked around the house in my pajamas, never having to get dressed. Some days, I never spoke a word to an adult until Greg came home; and when he deployed, my language skills greatly decreased as my used vocabulary was that of a toddler. Laundry and dishes multiplied and so did the tasks of motherhood to include driving, shopping, cooking, paying bills, helping with homework, breaking up fights, cleaning, and learning multiple sports. Well-meaning women who got paid for their work would sometimes ask me what in the world I found to do with my time all day. They soon regretted the question as I vehemently expelled the list of my day's activities. Sometimes, the mundane simplicity of my calling overtook my good judgment as I blubbered to God, "What am I doing? I have a master's degree." I was conflicted. I wanted to stay home full time with the boys, but I wanted to use my education also. When the boys started school, people suggested that now I work. But I explained my need to volunteer in their class, to be available for field trips, and to be home when they get home from school. When they started high school, the familiar voices repeated the same: "NOW you should go back to work." But how can I divide my life and be at every ball game and take them to practice? No matter what the outside world echoed, my heart was steadfast and my conviction unwavering—my call was to be a stay-at-home mom no matter how difficult at times.

I thought my place in this world was settled in my heart and mind, and the conflict resolved. But somehow, in moving from base to base, town to town, country to country, I lost me. We moved, and Greg had a place to go—work. We moved, and the boys had a place to go—school. I had chosen to be a stay-at-home mom, and I loved it, but it seemed that my place in the world was dependent on someone else's place. We moved, and I struggled to figure out where I had to go. What I had to do. I was Chaplain Woodbury's wife or Ben and Matt's mom wherever we went. Don't get me wrong. I absolutely love those titles, but I was not content with titles. I wanted an identity that gave contentment. I was confusing my role in life with identity.

Who am I? I grew up in South Carolina, in a home with two Christian parents, a brother, and a sister. I grew up pulling weeds in the garden on Saturday morning and on Saturday night eating a vegetable supper from that garden before baths and the studying of our Sunday school lessons. We held to strict rules of etiquette—no white shoes after Labor Day or before Easter and always, always say, "Yes, ma'am" and "No, ma'am. My grandmother, a genuine Southern Belle from the Charleston area, tutored us from the Amy Vanderbilt Book of Etiquette, even giving my husband a copy when we were engaged. She was careful to tell us that ladies should not speak loudly. So when she had something to say, which might be regarded as inappropriate for a lady, her hand would be on her heart, and she would lean and whisper. Our family was Baptist, so when Grandmamma met Greg, who I was seriously dating at the time, she approached my daddy with this concern, "But, Rudy (my dad), he's of a different faith!" Presbyterian! My dad lovingly reminded her, "mom, he is Christian."

Growing up, a big trip meant going to North Florida to see grandparents or the very occasional trip to the mountains of North Carolina or to Gatlinburg, Tennessee. So naturally, my cultural experiences were limited. I flew on my first airplane after my sophomore year in college in order to serve as a summer missionary. When I arrived at my location, I realized that things were so different there. People talked differently, and everything moved at such a fast pace. I was in VIRGINIA! At our first assignment in the military, which was in Georgia, I began to mingle with Air Force people from all over this great country, and I began to recognize palatable differences in people. We were attending a public function when another lady had the nerve to ask me in front of everybody if I dyed my hair. I was appalled, and with my best Southern indignation but with a smile and hand over my heart, I informed her, "I dye my shoes and color my hair."

We have lived all over the world, but I still have a very distinct Southern accent. When Matt was in kindergarten, he came home and informed me that I said his brother's name wrong. I knew I slaughtered phonetics, but I also knew that my firstborn would always be called "Bin" and not "Ben." When I lived in Colorado and New Mexico, people always guessed I was from Texas. That's the Southern they were accustomed to. I grew up in South Carolina, with Southern parents and customs, and I still put my hand over my heart and whisper, "Bless your heart," with the best of them. But being Southern is no more who I am than the roles of mother, wife, or social worker are who I am.

Who I am is determined by my relationship with the One who created me. When I repented and accepted Christ's sacrifice for my sin, I died to myself and was raised to live in Him. Christ lives in me, and THAT is my identity—nothing else. Not my background, not my job, not my husband's job, not who my children are, or what they are accomplishing, or not accomplishing. Galatians 2:20 says, "I have been crucified with Christ, I no longer live, but Christ lives in me. The life I live in the body, I live by faith in the Son of God who loved me and gave himself for me." The struggle over my role throughout my life is real, but as I grow in my understanding of my identity rooted in Christ, I am able to let go of external fears, concerns, expectations, and definitions of my life, and become free to experience every day whatever He has for me. "One thing" is all that is needed. So I began to define my life, my work, and my sense of who I am and what I do around that "one thing." I said to myself, "The Lord is my portion. Therefore, I will wait for him" (Lam. 3:24). He is all I need; I will find my worth, my place, my contentment in Him.

So we moved from place to place. With my identity in Christ, He could define my role. I didn't lose my gifts as a social worker just because I wasn't paid. He cultivated, enlarged, and multiplied them. Each time I moved, it was an opportunity to use whatever gifts God desired for that time and for that place. One assignment, I did lots of counseling with military and chapel folks. One assignment, I played keyboards and sang in the praise band at the contemporary service Greg created. Several assignments, I organized retreats and spoke at conferences. Most assignments, I taught ladies Bible study. But through all the assignments, I was directed, ordained, and cherished my role as mom! Because my "one thing" was Christ in me, I was better at being a content mom to my two little people. Because when I died daily to myself, my life wasn't all about me but could be about Greg, Ben, Matt, and the ministry around me. They were my target ministry. There will always be times of discontentment and many voices around expressing their opinion (I thank the Lord I am not parenting in the Facebook era), but we can learn to be content as Paul expressed that he had "*Learned* to be content in whatever circumstance" (Phil. 4:11; emphasis added).

We were stationed at a special operations base when Matt was in high school. Greg and Matt bantered back and forth with Greg's title. Greg reverently boasted that he was now a special ops colonel while Matt tried to denigrate Greg's role by saying, "Dad, you're a chaplain!" One spring afternoon, we took our usual places at the baseball field. Greg and I were up in the stands, and Matt was, that day, playing first base. The game was becoming a bit chippy, and Matt determined that he needed a strategy other than just playing good baseball to throw the opponent off their game. A runner from the other team had just reached first base when my six-foot-five son leaned into his opposition, who was by now greatly overshadowed by Matt's frame, and whispered these words of intimidation, "You see that real big man in the stands staring at you right now? That's my dad. He's a special ops colonel!"

Our various roles become very important and very useful at different times in our lives as we allow God to ordain them. We have a dining room suit that we had made in Turkey. I brought an Ethan Allan catalogue to the Turkish builder, and he built the exact table, chairs, and hutch I wanted from the catalog. None of which I could have afforded to purchase from a store in the United States. But as we have moved six more times since Turkey, our chairs are showing their character and their less-than-stellar quality. They are falling apart! I still like the way they look, but they are not functional unless after every move, we get out the gorilla glue and repair the weak portions. In our nomadic lifestyle—through moves, deployments, being away from family, changing schools, losing friends, changing churches, finding support, learning jobs—Greg has verbally blessed me with a precious role and a priceless identity. He said that I was the glue of our family! Now normally, I would not think it positive to be compared to "a hard, impure, protein gelatin, obtained by boiling skins, hoofs, and other animal substances in water, that when melted or diluted is a strong adhesive"; but in this case, I was honored.

What a mom does is not wood, hay or stubble! It's not real glamorous, it's very messy, it's sometimes extremely redundant, it's many times lonely. It won't get you any prizes, money, or tremendous affirmation. It demands great sacrifice. But as you pour your life into a person who grows and learns of God, through you, the results last forever, and the benefits package is priceless! At a yuppie restaurant one evening on date night, Greg and I found ourselves in a conversation with an artsy musician who was talking about cultural events and happenings that currently were not a part of our lifestyle. We listened and attempted to engage as he droned on about things of which we were not the least interested. Finally, as we excused ourselves from the conversation, he asked me a poignant question, "What is your most creative endeavor?" My children. They are my most creative endeavor. They are my gold, silver and precious jewels.

Walking through the halls of the Moody Air Force Base Chapel one Sunday in May of 1997, person after person after person greeted me with an affectionate, "Happy Mother's Day." Not yet understanding the tradition, my almost three-year-old son, Matt, looked up at me and asked why everybody was saying that to me. Stooping down to answer that sweet little question, I said, "Because God made me to be a mom, and we are going to celebrate!"

The Birth of a Man

The doctors were unaware that Matt would be born weighing ten pounds and eleven ounces. Thankfully, I was too. So when the time came for the final push, I was quite confused when my normally mild-mannered doctor began yelling intense instructions at the nurses and me in order to get Matt out. His head was out, but his shoulders and chest were very large, and seemed to be holding up the whole process. Finally, the shouting stopped, and the crying of a new baby began. Exhausted and in awe, I held this huge baby and thought as Eve said, "With the help of the Lord, I have brought forth a man" (Gen. 4:1). He felt like a man but looked like a baby. But this baby would become a man. To parent effectively, I had to set my mind on the reality that this huge yet small little person would one day be a man. How would I assist and support this process whereby this baby should become a man? I will PARENT, not just be a parent. And I would do so with intentionality and deliberateness, realizing the absoluteness that I did not just have a baby, but I had a future man—somebody's husband and somebody's daddy.

My mama always used to tell me that many times, she would look at my sister and me when we were little, and wonder what her little girls would become. I looked at my boys with that same wonder. But I realized that I had a big responsibility in molding who and what they would become. Whether I was looking at Ben or Matt, the question remained: "What kind of man would he become?" He would be a husband, he would be a daddy, and he would be a workman. It's as if at the birth of our children, we are given a mission. Not a mission impossible, but a mission that should we choose to accept, would prove rewarding, challenging, and intense, and would result in the making of an adult.

The Bible states our mission clearly: "He commanded our fore-fathers to teach their children" (Ps. 78:5b). To teach is to "impart knowledge, skill, or give instruction to" (dictionary.com). As soon as the baby is born, he is learning. And as soon as the initial trauma and trepidation of a baby at home alone with parents who don't know a thing about being parents has diminished, these two newbies start teaching. We start saying letters and sounds, contorting our mouth and exaggerating the enunciation of letters in an attempt to teach the baby to form sounds, then words, then sentences. When the boys were babies, as soon as they were standing even once, we put a cart with a handle in front of them to push around so they would learn to walk and eventually run. We, as most parents, sat on the floor, coaxing the boys to walk from parent to parent, clapping each time an extra stride was taken. The same intentional and deliberate process of teaching and learning was duplicated for eating, learning manners, learning the family rules, learning to read, learning to have friendships, learning to do chores, learning to study and do homework, learning to apologize, learning personal hygiene, learning to tell the truth. I am already exhausted with this incomplete list of concepts and skills we as parents are called to teach our children. We consciously and meticulously teach these to our children because we absolutely know they have to have these skills to grow and survive in the world.

While our intentionality is critical for these necessary life skills to develop in our children, as Christian parents, we are given a greater imperative to be even more deliberate in teaching our children Jesus. We thoughtfully, carefully, and eagerly teach our children to physically walk; but we carelessly just hope they will learn how to walk with God. We sometimes concentrate on the other knowledge to such a degree that we neglect our duty and fail our children by relegating the teaching of Jesus to Sunday school teachers, Awana leaders, or youth group leaders. Christian parents are commanded to teach our children about Jesus, and we must do so with the same or greater deliberateness and intentionality with which we teach other skills. We must choose to, decide to, plan to, and then do it. Immerse our children with right theology and doctrine, and then practice that theology at home as they grow. The world is very intentional and deliberate with teaching our children that which is against God, and the world will attempt to indoctrinate them with all that is wrong yet portraying itself as good. We have our mandate from scripture: "For I have chosen him so that he will direct his children and his household after him to keep the way of the Lord, by doing what is right and just" (Gen. 18:19). We are to teach the fear of the Lord, the gospel of Jesus, the way of wisdom and discernment, how to walk with Jesus every day, how to pray, how to study the Bible, how to be grateful, how to repent, how to do God's will. Yes, this too is an exhaustive yet incomplete list. Thankfully, the Bible does give us instruction on the how and when to teach. "Love the Lord your God with all your heart and with all your mind and with all your strength. These commandments that I give you today are to be upon your hearts. Impress them on your children. Talk about them when you sit at home and when you walk along the road, when you lie down and when you get up. Tie them as symbols on your hands and bind them on your foreheads. Write them on the doorframes of your houses and on your gates" (Deut. 6:5–9).

What that sounds like to me is that we as parents are first to love and worship God ourselves as a role model for our children to diligently seek God with all that we are. Some parents work from the theory that children will just follow their example. But we are called to let them see our example and actively lead them, not just hoping they follow. While doing so, we are to saturate our children with Jesus! If you saturate something, you soak it thoroughly and completely. Soak your home, your car, your activities, your speech, your entertainment with Jesus, with His Word. As Beth Moore put it, "Scripture is for how you do life" (*Stepping Up, a Journey Through Psalms of Ascent*, p. 131). As you play, teach Jesus. As you teach life skills, teach Jesus. As you leave the house or stay at home, teach Jesus.

Theology is the study of God. A forty-year-old can study God, and a two-year-old can study God. It is never too early to start teaching about Jesus. Paul shares the example of Timothy, "How from our infancy you have known the Holy Scriptures which are able to make you wise for salvation through faith in Christ Jesus" (2 Tim. 3:15) Sometimes they get it right, sometimes they struggle for understanding, and sometimes they teach us. As long as we are being intentional about our teaching and discussing, they will learn. One night, I was called into Ben's room to pray with him so he wouldn't be afraid. Then I was called into Matt's room to pray for him not to be afraid. After we prayed, Matt, who was three, explained, "There are two Jesus 'cause He is with Ben, and one is with me. No, there are four: one for me, Ben, you, and Daddy." That was a time to teach! Ben had a game when he was four where he would whisper very low and ask God if He could hear him. That was a time to teach! *Jurassic Park* is pretend," Ben explained. "God is real." That was a time to share! "You can find your joy if you read the Bible," Ben reassured us. That was a time for me to remember! Grabbing Matt's little toes, I said, "These are Mama's toes." He correctly chided me, "No, these are Jesus's toes." That was a time to rejoice!

Every night, we read colored-picture, Bible-story books to the boys. Ben lay still on the bed hanging on to every word, asking questions, pointing to the pictures, engaged in every detail. Matt fiddled with toys, played with my hair, loved and kissed on me or Greg, and sometimes even walked around. I wondered if this child would ever be interested in the things of God. Of course, he was only three. One day, someone at church mentioned a Bible story about Ahab and Queen Jezebel. Without skipping a beat, Matt began reciting the story verbatim as if he were reading it to us. Stunned at this display, I realized that it is never too early for children to hear God's word and thus, study God. I am responsible for the telling. The child WILL hear as I tell it over and over again in many different ways so that my little growing people will be saturated with the word of God.

I was trying to teach Matt the concept of our bodies being the temple of God. I felt if I began this teaching early (he was six) it would cause them to think before harming their bodies as they got into the teenage years with all the pressures that it would bring. I explained that his body was the temple of God. I asked if he knew what they meant. He said yes, that Jesus lived in him. Then he sheepishly smiled as he asked, "Does that mean I have lots of other people worshipping in me too?" The lessons to me that day are keep trying and don't give up. What they don't get now, they will eventually.

Every day, circumstances that occur in family life bring opportunities to teach right doctrine or right beliefs from God's word. My store-bought quilt was hanging over the rack and just below it, a pair of scissors. My gaze darted back to the quilt where I noticed a large cutout pattern that was not previously there. The two likely suspects rounded the corner where they were thoroughly interrogated. First Ben, who was six, delicately reported that he had seen Matt stand beside the quilt rack, and he had seen the scissors in his hand that day. Matt, who was four, upon confrontation, gingerly agreed that he "must have done it." When we took Matt to the bathroom to discuss a likely punishment, the guilt became too much for Ben to bear. He banged on the door and admitted that he had cut the quilt and blamed it on Matt. Sin, guilt, and confession are all very big concepts but easily understood in the light of life and God's Spirit saturating a family. And to Matt, the lesson was, "You don't have to confess to something you didn't do even if Ben says you did." Another lesson.

Ben thought I was absolutely nuts one day when he reluctantly aired a long list of items he needed to confess. He began by saying that he felt really, really bad and the things he had done bothered him greatly. Standing humbled and worried about my response, Ben was quite confused when I hugged him and kissed him, and with great effervescence, told him that this was a reason to celebrate. Baffled at my display of love, Ben questioned my understanding of what he had just revealed. Then I told him about the doctrine of the Holy Spirit and his conviction in our lives. I shared with him that because the Holy Spirit was working in his life, it was a testimony that he was a child of God. "Ben," I told him, "the Spirit convicts and by this proves you are God's child" (Rom. 8:16). That is something to celebrate. That is daily, teachable doctrine—even to children.

As for practicing our theology—well, we will do that until Christ comes back. Ben, who was prone to worrying, like his mom, was concerned about a math test. I began to talk to him about scripture and about not worrying but just studying and doing his best. He commented that he heard and knew what I was saying, but it sounded like a bunch of "blah blah blah." My child, with the words of Charlie Brown's teacher, voiced the reality that practicing what we know of God and His word is sometimes difficult in the midst of daily life.

Nevertheless, we continue to practice, and there are so many ways to practice good doctrine as you teach it to your children. Teach your children scripture and you will many, many times over see it play out in their lives, which becomes an opportunity to showcase the Living Word in their lives. For example the verse, "Everyone who exalts himself will be humbled, and he who humbles himself will be exalted" (Luke 14:11), led us through many athletic events. Ben had an ongoing competition with another baseball player that started in middle school and continued through high school. Both were catchers, but in the beginning years, the other boy was ahead of Ben in the lineup. As they approached high school tryouts, the other player touted to everyone at school that he would beat Ben out as he had done in the past. With this rumor circulating, Ben became angry and somewhat intimidated, but we encouraged him to practice very hard and not to say a word. He was to only speak of his playing ability though his actions on the field, not with his mouth. By the time tryouts were over, Ben was the lead freshman catcher and after only three games, was pulled up to junior varsity. The two boys continued their friendship through playing together and put the competition behind them. This example of scripture lived out, served as a great testimony to Ben and Matt as to the truth of scripture and the way correct doctrine can be practiced daily.

Our assignment as Christian parents is the same as in the days of Nehemiah when the Levites read the scripture to a standing audience: "They read from the Book of the Law of God, making it clear and giving the meaning so that the people could understand what was being said" (Neh. 8:8). So that's our charge: read the word to our children and explain it through our lives and in daily life so they will understand its meaning. As we enact this in real life, the questions will come, and the struggles will arise. I remember a conversation Matt and I had about nurturing his relationship with Jesus through daily devotions. I used the analogy that he grew closer to me by talking to me every day to which he replied, "But I see you always." He was right, but we were able to discuss the truth that to have a disciplined faith meant that you don't always see with your eyes.

When in middle school, Matt was furiously writing during the sermon one Sunday. I refrained from stopping him, and immediately following the service, he barraged me and Greg with a list of twenty-six questions he had compiled. Some of the questions were just vocabulary questions, some were obviously assembled by a middle-school boy, but there were some like these: "What is sovereign? How can it be that God hardens people? What kind of question is it to ask, 'Is God unjust?' How can you worship yourself? What is 'devine' (his spelling)? What is we can't get our arms around theology mean? What are vessels in our life? What are balls and strikes in our life? Or what does it mean that we are frail?" To be able to reason through these questions as a family is studying God together. It's living the scripture together, it's accomplishing our mandate from God, it's teaching our children.

While Ben was choosing a different college to attend with an ROTC program after a particularly difficult year at his first school, he came back to live at home for a short respite. One afternoon, he casually walked through the house and, upon finding me, asked a not-so-casual question. In fact, it was a question that impacted me so greatly that I wrote it in my journal and am repeating it to you years later: Will I teach my young adult son as I did my five-year old son? The answer is deliberately and intentionally YES! Flashing through my mind were the little boys with "air artillery" in their hands marching and singing, "I'm in the Lord's army." And the equally exuberant song and motions that surely aided in my knees going bad as we loudly proclaimed, "If you read your Bible and pray every day, you'll grow, grow, grow. If you don't read your Bible and pray every day, you'll shrink, shrink, shrink." For a split second, I reminisced about our daily family devotions and all the text message scriptures and every way we had found to teach and to saturate our boys with the work and word of Jesus. And now he asked, "Will you teach some more?" Absolutely, always and forever. I am your mom; that's my mission!

As a five-year-old little girl, I stood on my granddaddy's feet, held on to him as he held me, and while gently dancing around with me on his feet, he sang, "Daisy, Daisy, give me your answer true. I'm half-crazy over the love of you. It won't be a stylish marriage. I can't afford a carriage. But you'll look sweet upon the seat of a bicycle built for two." My granddaddy died when I was six, so I got on the feet of my daddy as he gently danced around and sang, "Daisy, Daisy…" When my boys were little, they climbed on the feet of me or Greg and asked, "Do Daisy, do Daisy." One day, maybe one of my grandchildren will climb on Ben or Matt's feet and say, "Daddy, do Daisy." The little dance is not of great importance, but it is of great worth because it was passed down. A simple moment passed down from generation to generation became a significant connection with my granddaddy and thus, his daddy who danced on his daddy's feet. This dance is not important to parenting, but the passing of what we know to generations that follow us is immensely important to God.

The word entrusted means that we have been given a responsibility or charge to care for something that was given to us. In 2 Timothy 1:14, we are cautioned to, "Guard the good deposit that was entrusted to you—guard it with the help of the Holy Spirit who lives in us." As a parent, one of the saddest and convicting statements in the Bible is found in Judges 2:10: "After that whole generation had been gathered to their fathers, another generation grew up who knew neither the Lord nor what he had done for Israel." One generation died. The next generation did not know the Lord. Who was responsible for that tragedy? The parents who were entrusted with these children and who were instructed to pass on to these children the knowledge of God, and who…. chose not to. Therefore, their children and the generations to come suffered the consequences. When we take our mandate to pass down the faith to our children seriously with deliberate intentionality, we are not only affecting our children, but also generations to come. Your life will be a blessing to your children, your grandchildren, and the children yet unborn. "What we have heard and known what our fathers have told us, we will not hide from our children, we will tell the next generation, the praiseworthy deeds of the Lord. His power, and the wonders he has done. He decreed statutes for Jacob and established the law in Israel which he commanded our forefathers to teach their children so the next generation would know them even the children yet to be born and they in turn would tell their children. Then they would put their trust in God and would not forget his deeds, but would keep his commands" (Ps. 78:3–7).

I remember as a little girl watching Billy Graham's crusades on TV with my parents. The message he spoke was simple and to the point. An invitation was always given, and hundreds and thousands would always respond. A couple of years ago, we were at the Cove for a Military Chaplain's Conference hosted by the Billy Graham Association. Will Graham, Billy Graham's grandson, spoke on behalf of his grandfather. He shared a simple but profound concept and insight into the ministry of his grandfather. He said we should always invite people to make a decision about what they have heard. I know that I am more likely to do something if I have been personally invited. But I have witnessed churches and families where God's truth was spoken and then, that was it. There was no personal invitation given so that someone was challenged to respond to the appeal. But Jesus always invited by saying, "Come." Our passing on of our faith to our children will only be complete when we invite them to experience the same relationship with Christ that we enjoy. We deliberately, and with great intention, teach them about Jesus and invite them to know him.

I love that as Paul met Timothy, he realized the truth of his mother and grandmother's faithful work of Christian parenting as he exhorted Timothy, "I have been reminded of your sincere faith which first lived in your grandmother Lois and in your mother Eunice and I am persuaded now lives in you" (2 Tim. 1:5). One ordinary spring evening after supper, when the boys were young, we took them outside to play. Ben jumped off the swing to run and tell us something that appeared to be of major importance to him. "Mom, when I was swinging, I looked up into the sky 'cause I love Jesus, and I was just thinking about that." That ordinary evening became an extraordinary celebration as a new generation was accepting the invitation to "come."

I invite you to commit to this greatest mission. "I will perpetuate your memory through all generations."

A Method to My Watering

In the farming community in South Carolina where I grew up, the farmers had a unique method of watering their crops. Each Sunday morning, before the offering plate was passed, a deacon stood up before the church and offered a prayer asking the Lord to provide rain for the fields. Many years later, after I was married and began moving around, I learned that people in different parts of the country used different methods of watering—different methods to make their grass or crops grow.

We moved to Albuquerque, New Mexico, which is called High Desert; and for the first time in my life, I encountered a foreign method of watering. Each lawn that wanted to remain green had an underground sprinkler system which thankfully was paid for by our landlord. I was appalled that people were actually paying to water the grass in their yards. When I asked the ladies at Bible study why people in New Mexico didn't just pray for rain, they said they had never considered that as an option. Several years later, we moved to Colorado and bought a house where we chose to employ both methods of watering. We had an underground sprinkler system, and we prayed for rain! Having a green lawn and trying to keep it as pretty as the neighbors was very expensive. Because I had two grow-ing boys, I relinquished the thought that I would ever be presented with the yard of the month sign and chose to buy groceries instead of excessive water for the grass. So I employed the praying method quite frequently. As I moved around to different parts of the country, I quickly learned if I was going to succeed at having a presentable lawn—not even a showcase lawn—I would have to use whatever method was necessary for that unique part of the country. Let's just say that I have learned more than I have desired about what it takes to make and keep grass green.

Yes, I learned there are lots of kinds of grass which will grow best in different kinds of climates and different kinds of soil. I know about my daddy's centipede, the green weeds in Albuquerque we called grass, the Kentucky blue grass that was a requirement of our Colorado neighborhood, the tall fescue we had in Clovis, New Mexico, and the beautiful lush grass of the tropical climate of Guam. I understand that children are different from grass, but I have learned that in order for children to grow as they were individually intended, different methods of "watering" also need to be employed.

My daddy was a forester and has a ton of knowledge and books on how to grow plants, but when my children arrived, I had no such book to study in order to learn how to get these little people to grow in a healthy manner. I was used to going to school, reading books, learning my job, and then heading out to perform my duty; but with this task, there were no practical books that were individually labeled—Ben or Matt. All I had was a little plump boy who cried, ate, smiled, and pooped! How was I supposed to know what he wanted when he cried? How he felt? What he needed? He couldn't tell me. So I did what I always did, I went to school. I studied my baby! The more I was with him, the more I understood what his whine meant, what his cry meant, or what his full-scale wail meant. I knew what he liked and what satisfied him. I learned all this before he was able to say a word because I paid close attention to WHO this little boy was, and what he craved and what he needed in order to grow.

My second son came along pretty quickly after the first one. A cavalier attitude of "I've got this. This is not my first," quickly turned to, "Help me. He's not like the first one," when I assumed that the same sound from this even plumper baby would mean the same thing it meant with my first son. It didn't take long for me to understand even these little babies, were very different from each other. They responded differently, they needed differently, they loved differently. So my education began again as I studied my new son.

Psalm 139:3 tells us that God is familiar with all our ways. He knows us in all our ways because He created us. God knew all about my boys as He was creating them in my womb before I even knew anything about them, so when I met them, I set out to know them and to become familiar with them in all their ways—all the ways that God had individually created them to be. Here is what I learned.

Ben is only a three-letter word, yet as a name and the person it represents, the word carries so much meaning. Born Benjamin Lloyd Woodbury in August 1992 to parents who had waited six years to have a child, Ben was also affectionately called Jamin. We learned very early of Ben's intensity and expressiveness. As Greg and my dad were setting up a new computer, our two-year-old son entered the room, spread out his little fingers wide and tight, and chided them emphatically to be careful because "that was VERY IMPORTANT to him." He was a bit bossy, even at two, but things and people are intensely important to Ben. I am so grateful that one of those is his brother Matt who came along twenty-two months after Ben. The first month we had Matt home, Ben was skeptical and surely jealous of this new attention grabber. He attempted to swat Matt and finally, out of frustration, exclaimed that he hated Matt. But soon after realizing this baby was here to stay, Ben became Matt's biggest helper, friend, and hero.

Throughout our military moves, they were best friends; and Ben was Matt's greatest coach, mentor, and protector. Ben made Matt a better athlete as Matt would always attempt to practice each sport more diligently just to keep up with his older brother. Early in high school, some kid was verbally abusing Matt. He came home one day and in disbelief, announced that the bully had made an unsolicited apology. Ben quietly slipped out of the room where we were hearing of this amazing change of heart. Later, I asked Ben if he knew anything about why the person had stopped harassing Matt. He calmly responded, "I might have made a phone call." I didn't ask any more questions, and Matt never knew about the incident. He did however know about another incident that occurred one afternoon at school after baseball practice. Ben was a junior, and Matt was a freshman who had been called up to pitch for the varsity team where Ben was the catcher. The team had been throwing snowballs after practice—baseball in Colorado—when Matt hit a senior who was not happy with this freshman pounding him. Later in the locker room, the senior jumped on Matt from behind, wrapped his arms around his neck, and began choking him. Ben, who was much lighter than the senior, grabbed him off Matt with nearly superhuman strength, threw him across the room, and unequivocally told him, "Do not touch MY BROTHER again!" Ben is fierce, steadfast, loyal, and completely dedicated to those people and things that are important to him.

As I studied Ben, I became very aware that there were two causes of his extreme intensity and sometimes angry outbursts. Before I understood completely Ben's dilemma, I watched my toddler run around the house with uncontrollable fits of what seemed like demon possession. One day, I just grabbed him and held on tight during the fit; and within minutes, my wild man gave up and fell asleep. That's all it was! He was tired and didn't know how to handle that need. So I learned and helped him negotiate his need for rest. But I had one more important concept to learn about Ben. We had a couple of blocks to walk home together every day after meeting the school bus during Ben's first-grade year. I immediately began quizzing him on the day's events. With very tempered speech and great self-awareness, he shut me down one day. "Mama, I am hungry and am starting to get the feeling of angry, so can we talk after my snack?" The knowledge of Ben's attitude when tired or hungry has enabled our family to bypass many an altercation.

Ben is an athlete and very competitive, yet quietly so. He began playing organized baseball at age three and also picked up basketball, football, and tried soccer. He loved baseball the best and eventually received a college scholarship as a catcher. While testing out his skills, Ben would never verbally say what position he wanted to play at first. But he worked and worked hard at a position until he knew he was able to play it well and someone else—the coach—would validate his work by offering him the job. That is my Ben—a quiet, hard-working competitor!

Some may say he is shy. Even before Ben's first day of first grade, he prayed, "Lord, I might be shy at first. Please help me not to be shy." But as Ben has grown, I realize he is cautious. He chooses his words carefully, and he observes. Some may say he is closed and guarded, but I see in him a sensitivity that comes from watching and learning. This has served Ben well as he exudes a quiet confidence and leadership that makes people want to follow him. You won't get too many words from him, but the words he speaks will have meaning.

True friendship is very important to Ben. During our first move, which took us from South Carolina to Moody Air Force Base in Georgia, Ben's number-one priority was to find a friend. Prior to moving, we had prepared him, and he had determined that all would be well with the move if he could only find one friend. So as we stopped for the night at a hotel in Valdosta, Georgia, before moving in, our two-year-old son approached the desk clerk while checking in and made a rather heartfelt appeal, "I've got to find some friends! Will you be my friend?" Ben is a friend that you would want to have. His peers have always loved him and rallied around him.

When you study your children, you learn, whether good or bad, that they may have adopted some of your traits. I learned early of two traits that I unfortunately contributed. Ben is somewhat of a perfectionist and sometimes a worrier. You noticed, for the sake of my personal esteem, I put, "somewhat" and "sometimes." This has been both positive and negative in Ben's life. He is very concerned about making good grades, and he applies himself diligently, but sometimes he has put too much pressure on himself to do things "just right." Ben cares greatly about his performance and can sometimes be regimented. He always wants to choose correctly. Teachers have always appreciated Ben. But Ben has had to learn that we want him to do his best; however, he doesn't have to be perfect.

Ben is a son with great intensity of emotion and love. He loves and cares deeply, yet in a quiet, faithful, dependable way. When I understood Ben's sensitivity and emotional intensity that he did not verbally express but outwardly displayed, I became a better mom to Ben. I was able to teach him to recognize in himself all of whom God made him and to communicate his emotions, needs, desires, and wants.

My son Ben is such a paradox. His intimidating look with big black eyebrows and a stern demeanor made him seem unapproachable, yet his big smile could—and has—melted many hearts. His quiet yet authoritative leadership that makes people follow him can sometimes mask the very deep and sensitive heart that prays fervently, cares deeply about people and their feelings, and can hardly pass a homeless person without giving. This is Ben—intense, loyal, protective, loving. I know this because for twenty-two years and counting, I have studied him, and I know him.

As a great surprise, twenty-two months after the birth of Ben, we had another son. Matt, a four-letter word, became the symbol of another four-letter word—love. Born in June of 1994, Matthew Cannon Woodbury would hardly be called by his given name again. His older brother, who had trouble with the pronunciation of the word, turned Matthew into Matt-Choo, which began an endless chain of names including Choo, Choo-Choo, Chewy, Chewbacca, and thankfully, just Woody!

Matt, weighing in at ten pounds eleven ounces at birth, entered the world physically large and never stopped growing. I studied how this obvious difference in size affected him, and by kindergarten, he began to realize the difference. Sad faced and confused, he arrived home from school one day and inquired, "Mama, was I held back?" Knowing he didn't even understand that term, I quickly replied no, delved deeper, and asked why he thought that. His reply was the beginning of his understanding that his size would distinguish him from others. "We were taking pictures and the teacher lined us up in a row." He then used his arm to motion what happened next. "There was everybody, everybody, everybody." Then raising his hand much higher in demonstration he stated, "Then ME."

Early in Matt's life, I failed to interpret some of his behaviors and thus, misunderstanding a great deal of who Matt is. As he sat on the mat during the first fifteen minutes of kindergarten, I proudly watched my excited son from the window before I gathered the courage to leave my "baby" with another woman. I noticed the teacher told Matt to move to a different area on the rug. He did not move. She asked again and he just sat there. After the third time, Matt happily picked his self up and plopped to another area of the rug as told. When he arrived home, I inquired as to why the teacher had to ask him so many times for him to finally sit in a different location.

With a big smile and slow drawl, he explained, "Oh, I was just day-dreamin'." It wasn't until the ninth grade that I officially learned that his daydreaming was attention deficit disorder. Matt has no part of the hyperactive portion of this disorder. In fact, he is very laid back. Because I was slow in interpreting his behaviors as illness, he received many unearned and misdirected punishments, but he gained many valuable coping and interpersonal skills. I learned that Matt is an easygoing overcomer!

What you see is what you get with Matt—open, friendly, talk-ative, talkative, talkative. His brother, a very different person than Matt, questioned many of his actions. As a fifth grader looking for a place to eat lunch in the cafeteria, Matt saw a grown man sitting alone. Matt asked if he could join him and proceeded to introduce himself, explain that he felt the man may be lonely, and ask questions about the man and his life. Nonchalantly that afternoon, Matt pro-ceeded to tell Ben that he had met the new middle-school principal that day at lunch. Ben's question, "Why would you do that? Why would you eat lunch with an adult you didn't know?" was met with a, "Why not?" Matt is a friend to everybody. Matt will talk to anybody young or old. He has skill that way.

Matt is quick-witted and sharp-minded, and has learned the art of getting what he needs, but in a polite manner. Let's not call it manipulation. Let's just say he is able to find the loopholes and help himself. My husband and I took Ben and Matt to a friend's house one night when Matt was about five so the daughter could practice babysitting under the supervision of her parents. I had informed the boys not to ask for food as that would be rude. Upon entering the house, Matt marched up to the father and articulated his dilemma, "If you want me to have something to eat, you are going to have to ask me." With that, the man opened his refrigerator for Matt's pleasure. Matt switched kindergarten teachers two months into the school year. On Matt's first day with the new teacher, she called on Matt to answer a question she had asked the class. "But I didn't have my hand raised to answer the question," explained Matt. With that answer, the teacher acknowledged he didn't have his hand up, didn't make him answer the question, and moved on to another student.

An unexpected proclamation came from my four-year-old Matt one night as I was getting him to sleep. "Mama, I'm gonna protect you. You know that's why God made me, to protect you." He affirmed this to his dad days later and continued to commit himself to the job. When he turned thirteen and realized that at six feet one inch tall he was already much taller than me, he professed again his calling with, "Mama, you are a lot smaller than me. I like that. Now I can REALLY protect you."

Matt's protector instinct comes from a zealous love that he HAS to demonstrate. He once shared his heart with me: "Mama, I love daddy and I love you, but I love you more just because you are weaker than daddy." His love is wide open, vocal, and tangible. His long arms and big body wrap me up in the tightest cocoon as he reveals his heart, "Mama, your hug is my favorite place to be."

Matt's personality is as big as his body. Everybody knows him and everybody loves him. He is never a stranger. His favorite song from an early age is "This is the day the Lord has made. Let us rejoice and be glad in it." And rejoice he does—through loud singing in the bathroom, in the shower, in the bedroom, in the kitchen. Wherever Matt goes, he carries a big dose of warmth that encourages us to love and to laugh. If you aren't laughing, he will attempt to remedy that with all manner of jokes, varied accents, and occasional imitations. Even Ben, with the strictest of discipline, can barely hold back the smile and even laughter that being with Matt elicits. My dad recalls when the boys were younger, they would always race each other. Ben was always faster, but if Matt could only get Ben to laugh while running, Matt could win!

My son Matt is big and strong, yet tender and loving. He lives in relationship and focuses on loving and being instead of "doing," which is sometimes hard for this type-A mom to grasp. My son Matt lives from the heart and is all present for everybody, all the time. I know this because for the past twenty-plus years, I have studied him, and I know him.

God's works are amazing. Here are two boys from the same parents, raised in the same home, yet they are so different. Ben has my thick hair and hobbit feet, but the rest of him looks just like his dad.

Matt has Greg's fine hair and rather large feet, but his face is definitely mine. Matt often complained that Ben was skinny and could eat all the Oreos he wanted while he was born with a dead metabolism. Ben, on the other hand, complained that he worked hard to gain even a pound while Matt seemed to be gifted with unnatural strength and ability. Matt often had problems with organization and exclaimed that he wished he could just be like Ben. From his vantage point, Ben could do anything. But as I heard this, I remembered just days earlier Ben lamenting that he needed to be more assertive. He stated if only he could be like Matt. The boys need only see as a mom sees after she studied them intently. They are different, but each one perfect as God intended.

I sneaked into the bathroom while Ben, at age eleven, was brushing his teeth. He was looking intently at himself in the mirror, making faces, widening his eyes as large as he could. He saw me and began a science lesson with animated excitement, "Mama, did you know that we see upside down and then our brain transfers the pictures around?' He whirled around with eyes wide open and said, "Look at my eyes. They are perfectly round." Then I shrieked as he began the boy adventure of crossing them and rolling them round in his head. "Mom, this is wonderful stuff!" Ben was expressing what I was learning: these children, these creations of God, are "wonderful stuff." Different from each other yet both wonderfully made.

Ephesians 2:10 says, "For we are God's workmanship, created in Christ Jesus to do good works which God prepared in advance for us to do." Romans 12:6 also states that we have different gifts according to what was given to us. God has given our children unique gifts, personalities, needs, and desires in advance for His purpose. We have to "train up a child in the way he should go" (Prov. 22:6). The way I watered the grass to make it grow looked very different in the lush tropics of Guam than it did in the dry plains of eastern New Mexico, but I studied and I learned what was required to make each lawn look its best. When I set my heart to study Ben and to study Matt, I learned how to individually nurture their particular heart and life for the growth and path that God had intended for them personally. I learned I could not discipline them the same and get the same result.

I learned that how I played with one, the other may not receive well. I learned that how I encouraged growth in one may be discouraging to the other. I had to become sensitive to who they were, who God made them individually. So I studied them, and God showed me how to nurture each of them in the particular way he should for God's glory and for God's purpose. I messed up many times when I forgot to parent for their particular needs but instead parented out of my own personality. As did the grass, they at times may have become brown or not as beautiful under that method of watering, but God is good and brings the rain back when we fail. So I got to study again.

Knowing the boys and their personalities, we often joke about the jobs that may not be suited for them. We determined that Ben, with his stern appearance, would not make a very good greeter—this is if you wanted the customers to actually enter the establishment. Matt ought not be a waiter—you would get lots of conversation but not much service. Thankfully, we know this. When stationed in Turkey, we took our base chapel youth on a retreat to Ephesus. The worship leader for the retreat, a phenomenal musician and friend, taught Ben and Matt a few chords on the guitar. The last night of the retreat before the worship time began, he invited the boys to come up on stage in front of all the teenagers to play their part with the rest of the praise team. To my five- and six-year-old boys, this was equivalent to playing in a million-dollar venue. They had rehearsed and were ready. Their instrumental version of "Hang on Sloopy" began. They played it perfectly and with great intensity; and as the teenagers stood, clapped, hooped, and hollered for my little boys, the two boys left the stage, but in very different ways. Ben did his best to ignore the crowd. He walked off the stage, ran to Greg, jumped into his arms and buried his head in Greg's neck. As Ben was running to Greg, Matt sashayed his way through the crowd, down the middle aisle, head up, high-fiving each adoring admirer. My two precious boys. Each different. Each created in the image of God. Each needing a mom to know them individually so they can grow as God intended when God thought of BEN and MATT.

A Pair of Cleats

The gospel of John uses the Greek word Paraclete as the name to describe the Holy Spirit. The word in Greek literally means, "to come along side of." In English, the word is pronounced, "*PAR-uh-kleet.*" As a baseball mom, I heard that sound and automatically thought of something with which I was very familiar—a pair of cleats.

Every baseball season, starting when the boys were three and four, the day came when we all loaded in the van for the great excursion. Greg, with more gusto and eagerness of a young boy getting his first pair, jumped in the front to drive and be in command of our enterprise. The boys, chattering about colors, styles, and brands, piled in the back of the van with great excitement and anticipation. And me? Well, with checkbook in hand, all the way to the store, I attempted to review the reasons why we should acquire reasonably priced cleats. After all, they were just young boys, not pro players.

We passed by all the stores I suggested we go to first and pulled into the stores from which Greg considered worthy of buying cleats. The three boys beamed as they ran in the store, knowing they would conquer this store and come out victorious with boxes in hand. You see, their dad was one of those boys, and he would make sure of one thing—they would have the right cleats. My pocketbook and I did not have a vote in this matter. When Greg was a young boy, he experienced a tragic event in the eyes of a little athlete that forever impacted our baseball season. For whatever reason, during one pee-wee-league football game, Greg wore tennis shoes and not cleats. As the story goes, Greg was a tight end, and the play was an end-around sweep. The ball was handed off to him, the path was wide open for a touchdown, not a player around within ten yards, and then the worst happened. As Greg turned the corner, he hit a sandy spot; and because he had on tennis shoes and not cleats, he slipped and fell. No touchdown. The rest of the game, he was outfitted with a pair of borrowed cleats.

Through the years, I learned the importance of the cleat to the football and baseball player. This equipment is vital to the performance, security, and the assurance that one had everything needed to succeed in the game. The very presence of the right cleat can make a difference in play. So I am told. I guess you could say that the cleats "come along side" the player to empower him to play—to win.

In John 14:18, Jesus said that He would not leave us as orphans, but He would come to us. The disciples were worried they had given their lives to be on this mission with Jesus and now He was talking about leaving, and they didn't fully understand. Therefore, Jesus comforted them by explaining that he would never leave them. The Counselor, the Spirit of Truth would be with them forever (John 14:16). He was outfitting them with a permanent pair of cleats—okay, Paraclete—to help them win the race set before them.

The Holy Spirit is God's Spirit who lives in those who have put their trust in Jesus. He is always with us. Jesus told his disciples that it was to their benefit that he would leave so that the Comforter could come. The Spirit is truth, so we can trust Him. The Spirit guides us in the Father's will so we can follow Him. The Spirit is always with us so we never have to be afraid. We can always be secure.

My six-foot-five, two-hundred-and-something-pound child came home from college for the weekend one day, held me close—almost smothering me—sighed serenely, and commented, "This is my favorite place to be, in your hug." Why would that be? I certainly could not protect him or guard him; but in that hug, he knew the security of my presence, just my being there, coming alongside his journey through life. In contrast, my older son is less demonstrative with his emotions, yet he calls maybe at midnight, maybe at four in the morning, and requests prayer. He knows I can't DO anything for him while he is in South Carolina and I am in Illinois, but he has security in my presence. He knows that security of having someone come alongside of him in his life journey. It is a promise I made by giving him life. I would never leave him as orphan.

This coming alongside of our children and providing for them the security of our presence looks different and acts different throughout their life. Did you ever crawl around on the floor peeking at your baby as they lay crying in the crib? Did you ever peer with one eye into the window of the baby nursery at church because, like Matt, your child began to wail as soon as they were handed off? I did. They cried and wailed because they sensed a separation of that security of presence that had already begun to form.

Boy, did my feathers get ruffled one day at Vacation Bible School. I know that's not what you would expect to hear from a chaplain's wife, but we have our moments, especially when it involves our children. I was teaching an older group of children when my toddler accidently saw me in the hall, and jumping out of his line, ran to me. I scooped him up for a second to hold him, hug him, and thus assuring him that all was good. But I was quickly reprimanded by a lady who said I was not a good mother because I was smothering him and not allowing him to grow independently of me. Now we all have our parenting opinions, but he was two years old! And no, he will not grow independently of me; but he will grow best within the nurture, security, and safety that my presence provides. He will grow best because we come alongside of *him*.

School posed many situations for me to come alongside of my boys. But, I never dreamed that my assistance would begin by helping my kindergartener who was kicked off the bus. We lived in Turkey where Ben and Matt absolutely loved to ride the Air Force Blue Bird bus to school. Until one day, when Matt got kicked off! Apparently, Matt, who often pointed to things with his middle finger, was pointing out something to the bus monitor who immediately and without regard to common sense, kicked him off the bus for shooting her the bird. Matt had no idea what she was talking about or what he was accused of doing. By the time I consoled Matt and confronted the hasty bus monitor, she realized that I was a mom who was coming alongside her son.

Throughout their school years, Ben and Matt, as all children do, had to go through ups and downs, good times and bad. They had to work through issues many times without my intervention.

Moving every two to three years was somewhat difficult on the boys, but also gave them instant skills that others did not acquire early. When going to a new school, I remember not walking down the hall with the boys, but walking in the distance. They would enter their classroom, and I would peek in the small window in the door just long enough for them to see me and give a slight nod. I never had to speak or help except to let them know that I was there. I was always there, and the security of that presence created a safe place to grow, a safe place to share, and a safe place to mess up.

"We are fam-i-ly" has been our family cheer since the boys were little. We all put our hands in the middle, piled up like the muske-teers, and chanted the words loudly. While our four hands clasped together as one, we then raised up together in the middle in a triumphant display of unity. Because we had built a safe place for the boys to know security, they were able to navigate a sometimes harsh world with mean kids, harsh teachers, or unfair coaches. The boys left for college, and each of them had often called home—or texted home recounting the mantra, "We are a team," right? The words may have changed slightly from, "We are fam-i-ly" to reflect a more grown up sound, but the sentiment remains the same: we need you, our parents, to be there for us to provide that security of your presence in which we find safety and joy.

Matt is now coaching baseball, and Ben has a son that will soon play baseball; so they will still depend on a good pair of cleats. But more than a shoe, we have the Paraclete, the Spirit of God, our counselor, our constant help. We as parents can only mimic a small amount of the security of presence to our children that God has provided us through His Spirit in which we find unlimited safety, unlimited joy.

Psalm 16:8–9, 11 says, "I have set the Lord always before me. Because he is at my right hand I will not be shaken. Therefore my heart is glad and my tongue rejoices; and my body will also rest secure because you will not abandon me to the grave. You have made known to me the path of life you will fill me with joy in your presence with eternal pleasures at your right hand." Ben was baptized in the Jordan River by his dad. It was an amazing experience for both dad and son just as Jesus's baptism in the Jordan River was an amazing experience for that original Father and Son. That night before going to bed, Ben prayed and thanked Jesus for allowing him to be baptized where He was baptized, and then he paused and questioned Jesus, "But I thought a dove was supposed to come and light on my shoulder?' He did Ben! You have the Paraclete!

I'll Fight for You

Matt could hardly wait for his turn to go to school. Watching Ben everyday getting on the big-boy bus and heading off to fun, excitement, and whatever else Matt conjured up that school would be finally paid off. It was his turn! He was ready to learn, and being a head taller than all his classmates, it was not a minute too soon!

Day after day, I asked Matt what he learned in school that day. He knew what he should be learning because every day at home, prior to him going to school, we read, learned numbers and letters, and talked about all the exciting new things he would learn at school. His daily response to my question was, "We played." One day, he asked a pointed question for a five-year-old boy, "Mama, when am I going to get to learn something? When will I read?" I did what any mother would do. I marched down to the school to visit his classroom. I found unorganized chaos cloaked as the new learning style of play. So I walked across the hall to observe another classroom where I found eager and receptive students learning and a teacher teaching.

Therefore, I began to fight. Going through the appropriate channels, I first addressed my concerns with the teacher. Upon learning that she did not intend to teach the children to read, nor did she read to them, except from food labels, I proceeded to the principal. There I was told of this new learning style that supposedly had great results. The children would play, and they would catch the concepts they needed along the way. Matt was great at catching any kind of ball, but I knew he would not just "catch" the knowledge he needed to learn to read or do math. I then took the fight to the superintendent of education where I questioned a system where a five-year-old begs to be taught, and the teacher just says, "Go play." After a group meeting with all the parties, including the teacher, the committee decided Matt could be moved to the classroom across the hall where teaching and learning were esteemed. The stipulation for Matt to be able to change was that the record could not reflect that the teaching method was flawed but only that my child was unable to learn within that particular system. I did not care how they had to justify the move; I just wanted the best for Matt. And I had to fight for it!

After Ben's illness, as a ten-year-old, we had to regularly go to the hospital to get his blood pressure checked. He had contracted poststreptococcal glomerulonephritis a couple of weeks before our move to Guam. I am not a medical person at all and knew very little about the process of taking one's blood pressure until this incident with Ben. The specialist who treated Ben prior to our move taught me to make sure the clinician that was taking Ben's blood pressure for monitoring and reporting back to him in the States took his pressure manually using a child's cup. The first time after moving to Guam that we went to the clinic to begin the monitoring process for Ben's blood pressure, I noticed they were not following these guidelines. I quickly but politely spoke up and asked that they use a child's cup and that they take his pressure manually. I was reprimanded and told not to question the medical profession and their ability to care for my child. You can imagine that I did not allow this intimidation to stop my continued pressure on the medical staff to correctly monitor my son as his specialist required. I had to fight for Ben when he could not.

First grade, third grade, fifth grade, eighth grade, every grade we dealt with the same issues with Matt in school. The teachers always loved Matt and helped him, but they always reported the same issues: he mentally leaves the classroom, he just doesn't do his work when the other kids do theirs, and he doesn't turn in a lot of his homework. Matt always made the honor roll, and the teachers commented on how smart Matt was and how he was always able to intelligently speak about the information that was presented. But Matt struggled tremendously! He spent hours and hours doing work that should have only taken a small amount of time. He always did his work but did not have the ability to keep himself organized enough to get the work to the teacher. I don't want to tell you about his middle-school locker that we eventually had him stop using. Matt was punished more times than I could count for missing assignments, not turning in work he had done, not listening to the teacher, not bringing home paperwork, and the list went on and on. Every teacher conference, the answer to my concerns about Matt was given by the teachers: "Don't worry. Matt is doing fine. He is just a boy!" While those words may have comforted us temporarily, it was no answer to my child's struggle. Matt prayed that something would be wrong with him because he felt stupid and slow. The first semester in high school, the task of school plus being a three-sport athlete became overwhelming, and I could see that something else had to be going on with Matt. He, as well as I, could not understand why he could not get organized or why he could not do what he truly wanted to do.

After discussions with all his teachers, we decided Matt needed to be tested for learning disabilities. Then the real fight began. We made calls to the school administrator, the insurance company, and several doctors, and finally saw the school district psychologist. Surprisingly, I left many of these conversations hearing the same platitudes: he is doing well in school, it is good for him to learn to work hard, and we will just seat him in the front of the room. The most ludicrous comment from a "school professional" emboldened my fight: "We have so many students to take care of!" So in my head, I yelled, and out loud I said, "But I have this one child who is NOT DOING FINE and who needs help. And I will fight for him!" So we did. Matt was diagnosed with attention deficit disorder and had many accommodations and medication that were proving very effective. He thanked the Lord that he was not stupid, and learned to feel like the smart person that God created.

Moses in Exodus told the people not to be afraid of the Egyptians, "The Lord will fight for you, you need only to be still" (Exod. 14:14). Our children must KNOW that we will fight for them. You can hear in David's words in Psalm 35:1–2 that he is begging God, "Contend, O Lord, with those who contend with me, fight against those who fight against me. Take up shield and buckler, arise, and come to my aid." Our children may not verbally ask us to fight for them, but they should be confident that we will. Joshua 23:10 records that, "one of you routs a thousand because the Lord your God fights for you just as He promised." No matter how big the obstacle we fight. "The Lord your God who is going before you, will fight for you, as he did for you in Egypt, before your very eyes" (Deut. 1:30) I want to build in my children that trust and confidence that as they see me fight for them, they know that I am on their side, just as I promised. It is not someone else's job to fight for my child, and very likely, no one else would anyway. "Do not be afraid of them, the Lord your God himself will fight for you" (Deut. 3:22). God himself fights for us and what a perfect parenting example.

I know what you are thinking: we need to teach our children to fight for themselves, to stand firm themselves, to be responsible for themselves and not just looking for someone else to bail them out. I absolutely agree! With parental supervision, we teach our children to learn how to stand up, be assertive, and learn to fight for themselves. We teach them that God does not call us to fight without first equipping us for the battle: "Therefore put on the full armor of God, so that when the day of evil comes, you may be able to stand your ground" (Eph. 6:13).

It didn't take us, as Ben's parents, very long to identify that he needed to be much more assertive with adults. We often joked when Ben wanted Matt or us to intervene in a situation on his behalf that this was his opportunity to gain skills. Later, we just said, "skillage," and everybody knew we were giving whichever boy at the time the opportunity to practice growth on their own. As other parents would go and talk to the child's coach on behalf of the child, we told Ben that he would always first have to advocate on his behalf with the coach. To equip him, we would role play the scenario, having Ben practice what he would say and how he would approach the coach. He was nervous and a bit petrified at times. His words may not have been intelligible to the coach, but Ben was growing and learning. He was equipped, and he had strength in knowing he had back up—mom and dad. God is our strength—our equipper—and our mighty back up.

The phone rang one afternoon in Guam and on the other end was a panicked Major asking if this was the chaplain. Evidently, Matt, who was nine or ten at the time, had a twelve-year-old boy on the ground with Matt's foot firmly placed on his head, instructing the bully never to tease him again. The Major instructed us that the older boy who was with Matt ran away. That was Ben, surely coming to tell us. In Clovis, the first story about Ben's broken fist that we heard was that he was mad over something and hit a telephone pole out of anger. The true story, we later discovered, was that some guys were at the house when we were not there, and one became rowdy and "disrespected" the house and would not leave. Ben broke the guy's nose. I obviously don't condone my boy's fighting, but to the bully and the brazen, sometimes you need to fight (maybe not physically).

I have never had to literally "put up my dukes" for my boys. They would laugh and just call my fists a small finger sandwich. But as God does for His children, I will fight for them when necessary! We are taught these two truths in scripture: God fights for us and we only need to be still, and God equips us to fight and goes with us. So for Ben and Matt, I equip them to fight for themselves, and I am always prepared to fight for them when necessary. As parents, our task in every situation is to ask for the wisdom to know which one to do—fight, or be back up!

He Stood on the Wall—for Me

Everyone in the military is familiar with TDYs. They are temporary duty assignments where the military member is away for a work assignment that lasts a week or two or five or six—just not long enough to be called a deployment. During this time, our boys always enjoyed some special privileges like everybody sleeping in mom's room. The exception to that privilege for me was if the TDY was more than a week. Then, everyone was back to their own room and a different treat was enacted for the remaining weeks of daddy's absence.

So there we were, ready for bed one weeknight during another TDY. My nine-year-old, Ben, was camping on a pallet at the foot of my bed; and my seven-year-old, Matt, was propped up on the California king, spouting off dad-like commands. Devotions were read, prayers were said, teeth were brushed, and everyone was tucked in when the phone rang. On my way out of the room to answer the phone, I finalized our goodnights with an affectionate, "I love you," and a firm, "Now go right to sleep." In our home, there are degrees of *doing* things and degrees of *being ready* to do things. For example, one may be ready to go to bed, but when you are RIGHT ready to go to bed—time's up—you had better be in bed!

Even though I left the boys with that ultimate instruction, I still heard squeals, shrieks, and laughter erupting from my room throughout my entire phone conversation. I could hardly listen to the person on the line for wandering thoughts of destruction and mayhem. When I was finished with the phone, I had just begun with the boys! I marched down the hall with great motherly indignation ready to dispense punishments. After serious investigations, I judged my oldest son, Ben, GUILTY! Frustrated by their lack of obedience and poor judgment, I quickly pronounced his sentence, "Ben stand on the wall for twenty minutes!" The boys knew this punishment, similar to time out, meant standing straight up, arms by your side, with your nose right up against a wall.

In my haste, I had pronounced a twenty-minute sentence, which is a long time for anyone to stand up against a wall, let alone a nine-year-old boy who should have already been asleep. Ben began to faithfully serve his time, but I was plagued by the fact that Ben's greatest need at that moment was to be in bed. After all, it was a school night, and regardless of his wrongdoing, he needed to go to sleep. But he was guilty, and the punishment had to be satisfied. Then I realized that both could be accomplished. "Ben, go to bed," I instructed. "I will stand on the wall for you."

Ben protested and told me I couldn't do that, but I lovingly nudged him toward the direction of my room and took his place on the wall. There I stood, in my house in Albuquerque, New Mexico, late at night, all alone with no one looking; and I thought, *Where did I get this wild hair?* For those of you unfamiliar with that lingo, it means, *Where did this crazy idea come from that I should stand on the wall in place of my son, taking his punishment as if it were my own?* But I continued to stand, arms straight by my side, nose to the wall, following all the rules of the prescribed punishment. For some reason, I was quite embarrassed, quite humiliated. No one could see, no one knew, except Ben. He crept around the corner once more, pleading that I not do this, arguing that he should be standing there. Again, I prodded him to bed and said, "Ben, you don't have a choice. I am doing this for you."

Twenty minutes is a very long time when you are standing at attention at a wall. After my fleeting thoughts of humiliation left, my mind always wandered back to Ben. I thought of him while standing on that wall. I thought how much I loved him. I thought of him sleeping peacefully on the pallet in my room, and I cried. I thought of Ben. After his sentence had been fulfilled, I went to my bedroom to kiss him goodnight once more. As I kissed him, his eyes opened, and I informed him that his time was served. It was finished. With tears in his eyes, and with as much love as a nine-year-old could muster, he grabbed my neck, held me tightly, and whispered, "That's just what Jesus did. I love you, Mama."

Ben, my least affectionate child, had experienced something that night. He got it. Ben loved me more that night than ever before because I had loved him in a way that he could not have conceived. I walked down the hallway alone, again thinking about what Ben had said: "That's just like what Jesus did." "While we were yet sinners, Christ died for us" (Rom. 5:8).

Now I know where I got that wild hair from. God wanted to use me to show Himself to my son. I learned a valuable lesson that night. My job as a parent is to model Jesus to my sons in a way that they get it. I know, and they know, I won't always do it right; but in the relationship of parent to child, we have an awesome privilege and an enormous responsibility to show Jesus. When Ben got it, when he experienced that love, he responded with love.

There are so many ways to teach Jesus to our children. We read the Bible, we tell them stories, we sing songs, and we take them to church. But when they see Jesus in us, they can experience Him first-hand, and they can respond. An intimidating fact of parenting is that not only do our children see and respond to what we do, but that they also mimic what we do. We model behavior. They do the same behavior. When Ben was four, he had an accident while playing around Papa's (my daddy) boat propeller. Before our next visit, I reminded him not to play hide and seek around the boat. He immediately shot back with an astounding truth, "Mama, talk to Papa too. Sometimes I copy him, ya know." That truth that Ben was now able to verbalize was very obvious to us several years earlier. Before Greg was able to come on active duty as a military chaplain, he had to be endorsed or appointed by the Southern Baptist Convention and thus, became a Southern Baptist Home Missionary. He had a beautiful commissioning ceremony at Ridgecrest Baptist Conference Center. After the ceremony, Greg made a call on a pay phone, long ago, on the grounds in front of that glorious chapel. Distracted by Greg's conversation, I missed Ben for just a minute, but quickly found him in all his glory. He had pulled down his little pants and had begun going to the bathroom right there on the front grounds of

Ridgecrest in front of God and all the new missionaries. Determined not to allow this exhibition to scar Greg's new standing with the Home Mission Board, I quickly proceeded over to help Ben with his pants and asked him what in the world possessed him to go to the bathroom outside. His words haunt me today, "But sometimes Papa goes outside behind the barn."

The truth is that our children copy us; they mirror what they see us do. Pictures speak over and over this truth. The pictures of Ben in Greg's military boots or the pictures of Matt in his high-top basketball shoes depict the desire of these two little boys to walk in Dad's shoes—to be like Dad. For parents, it is much easier sometimes just to tell children what to do, how to behave, how to love, and how to live. We behave similarly to Ben when they were both very young, and Matt was quite discouraged trying to clean his room. When I asked Ben to go help his little brother pick up his room, he offered these words, "I think the best thing I could do for Matt is to tell him to 'believe in yourself' and 'you can do it.'" We often follow this childlike stunt in our approach to parenting by thinking we can just tell them how to be. But as you guessed, that advice from Ben did not help Matt feel less discouraged about his room. Our children don't listen to words we say as much as they hear what we do and who we are. This song by Phillips, Craig & Dean has a great suggestion for us:

> Lord, I want to be just like you
> Cause he wants to be just like me
> I want to be a holy example
> For his innocent eyes to see
> Help me be a living Bible, Lord
> That my little boy can read
> I want to be just like you
> Cause he wants to be like me.

Scripture is full of admonitions for us to have the same attitude as Christ (Phil. 2:5) and to be imitators of Christ. In 1 Corinthians 11:1, Paul says, "Follow my example, as I follow the example of

Christ." Ephesians 5:1 states that we are to "Be imitators of God, therefore as dearly loved children." In Philippians 3:17, Paul advises us to "Join with others in following my example, brothers, and take note of those who live according to the pattern we gave you." The word "pattern" means an original or model considered for or deserving of imitation. God has given us His pattern in Jesus Christ who deserves our imitation. "The Son is the radiance of God's glory and the exact representation of his being" (Heb. 1:3).

There is no way we as human parents can fully imitate Christ nor can we parent as God parents us, in perfect love, mercy, grace, and justice. However, we have the word of God that is alive and active in us, and shows us the character of God; and we have the Spirit within us who gives us the same power that raised Christ from the dead. I have messed up many times, and by asking the boys to forgive me, I modeled our relationship with God. Where do our children get the concepts of mercy, grace, forgiveness, love, patience? Where do they learn the characteristics of God that we so want them to know and to emulate? When Matt was very little, I recall him looking up at Greg and asking, "Daddy, will you teach me to be like you?"

Several months ago, Matt and I were talking, and I asked him now as a twenty-year-old, "What makes a man a spiritual leader in his home?" He thought a minute and replied, "It's not so much what you say, Mama. It's who you are and what you do." Now where do you think he learned that? His daddy!

When the boys were very little, my mama and daddy were visiting, and my mama was tucking Ben in at night. Before the lights were turned off, as she bent down to kiss him, he looked at her very bewildered and commented, "You look like my mama." You see, Ben was just realizing there was a visible family resemblance. I pray every day my boys can see a visible family resemblance and one day say to me, "You look like Jesus."

I Can Be More Undignified Than This

Many days, the boys and I could be found jumping around the house, shouting to the top of our lungs with music blaring, flailing our arms—as to dance—repeating, "I can be more undignified than this." It's true; we could be. The line we repeated was from a popular Christian song based on the scripture in 2 Samuel 6:21b–22 where David, praising the Lord in a manner some felt unbefitting a king, says, "I will become even more undignified than this." In our home, unlike David, we kept our clothes on, but we often exemplified David's next line in scripture which says, "And I will be humiliated in my own eyes." With that humiliation came fun and uproarious laughter that produced an environment of joy that permeated our family. This precedent of fun, crazy laughter, and joy started even before the boys were born.

In Seminary, Greg and I lived the high life in a two-bedroom Seminary apartment on campus. One morning, I had not yet left for class and was in the back room. Greg had already attended his first class and bolted into the apartment, unaware of my being home, so I kept him unaware for some time. We had only been married a short time, and I had never heard Greg be so uncontrolled in joyful song. But this morning, with just himself and God, so he thought, he belted loose and became quite undignified. "Country Roads" took on a new tune as he proudly bellowed forth each line with great enthusiasm. When he finally reached his extra loud ad-lib portion, "Country roooods," I was crumpled up on the floor trying to contain a belly laugh that began to hurt with each new note of his song. He finally found me balled up in a fetal position and face red from enjoyment. He was humiliated in his own eyes, but as we came to conclude, it didn't matter. It was fun! It was silly! And that was just the beginning.

Children and laughter just go together. When the boys were babies, we would do the silliest things just to make them laugh. Greg would bring out the "tickle monster" or zerbert their bellies, and everybody would laugh so hard. Then came the little voice that kept it going, "Do it agin." So we did. You know you have done it too. You have humiliated yourself in your home many times just to get your babies or children to laugh. And when they laugh, you laugh, and then you repeat so it will continue. We just want the joy to continue, so in our home, we devised a scheme. Our bed became the boat, and there were alligators all around the boat; so everyone would stay on the boat and laugh and play, and the joy kept going! The call "everybody to the boat" was met with screams of fun, laughter, and running to the big bed.

The scripture says that "our mouths were filled with laughter and our tongues with songs of joy" (Ps. 126:2). We didn't plan that our family fun and laughter would be a testimony to the Lord, but it was. When joy that the Lord gives overwhelms, fun and laughter can be the overflow, and singing comes! Not "Country Roads," but all manner of other songs that saturated our home with Jesus and became an avenue for lively, boisterous, yet effective teaching.

As toddlers, the boys played soldier (airmen), identifying with Daddy as they flew around the room and marched, loudly singing, "Onward Christian Soldiers" and "We're in the Lord's Army." Singing became a spontaneous interactive communication between me and the boys where I could burst out in an unrehearsed "Jesus Loves Me" or a quiet, "You are my sunshine, my only sunshine." Through the fun and laughter of the song, the boys learned scripture and did as the man healed in Acts 3:8, lots of "running and jumping and praising God."

The boys grew, our songs got louder, the dancing and singing became more aggressive, and the joy continued. Carman became our favorite singer, and we performed quite unrestrained right along with him. Yes, humiliation and hilarity ensued in our own home, and the boy's choice was a competitive chorus of, "I love Jesus, yes, I do. I love Jesus, how 'bout you?" What started as a nice song became a chant, then a contest, then—you guessed it—a shouting match. But I believe Jesus was pleased with the words of our mouth expressing, whether consciously or not, their love for Him. As the boys learned to "shout for joy to the Lord, worship Him with gladness, and come before Him with glad songs" (Ps. 100:1–2) in our house, that expression of love for Jesus would more easily be carried outside the house wherever they went.

Ben was ecstatic to see that even the mall was marked by a Carman song we had learned at home. The song started with the question, "Whose in the house?" and ended with the answer, "JC— Jesus Christ is in the house today!" With his little eyes beaming, he pointed to the side of JC Penny and exclaimed, "Jesus Christ is here too!" Ben understood that we sang that song at our house to proclaim Jesus's presence with us, so after his innocent declaration with nothing more to add, I concurred that Jesus was everywhere. We started singing in the car, and then we walked right into Jesus's store.

Ecclesiastes 3:4 tells us that there is "a time to weep and a time to laugh; a time to mourn and a time to dance." So in our time of undignified fun at home, we added dance. We were not, however, expecting Matt to take this form of praise outside the house, but he did! Ben and Matt, who were nine and seven at the time, were sitting together sweetly on the front row of the church during praise and worship before their dad was to preach. I was playing keyboard on the stage when out of the corner of my eye, I caught sight of the "dance" lady approaching the boys. Ben, tensing up and trying to ignore her, courageously resisted her encouragement to take the ribbons and dance. Then I saw Matt. His eyes gleamed as the "dance" lady came closer and closer. He was sitting on the edge of his seat, waiting with anticipation. Though we had told the boys not to take the ribbons because the "dance" had become quite a disruption, the temptation overwhelmed Matt, and he excitedly grabbed the ribbons and took off running and "dancing" around the room, furiously waving his "praise" ribbons. Ben sat mortified. I banged louder on the keyboard, hoping Matt would look at my stern-mom face. And

Greg, well, I think he just bowed his head, pretending to be in prayer before he preached. Even though Matt got in quite a bit of trouble that day, his dance could not be thwarted. His presentation of the "Worm" in ninth grade Latin class landed him a busted and bleeding belly button, and the dance circles in which he and his high school basketball team engaged themselves awarded him much notoriety around many gyms in New Mexico.

Undignified fun in our home was not just about singing and dancing, but about laughing, being silly, and just creating joy! These crazy fun times were about making memories and about creating a connection. A connection just happened to include horseplay, clowning around, joking, with lots of good times and laughter— loud laughter! These festive treasures came from simple amusements. Silly names like doogy-head, or buggy-head, exploding from the mouths of toddlers, snow dances that had to be performed ritualisti- cally by middle school boys to cause a snow day, or a mom who had daily song-and-dance performances at lunch to keep little boys enter- tained while eating. As the boys grew, the amusement expanded. The medallion game became a favorite. I would stand in the middle of our Turkish rug which had a medallion in the center. With legs tense and all muscles called on to help out, I would try to stand my ground while the boys attempted to push me out of the medallion—tackle football style. Thankfully, Ben and Matt grew up too quickly for that game to be viable much longer, so we switched to, of course, what everyone would go to, taking turns jumping up, trying to touch the doorposts of our den that had ten-foot ceilings. Was I ever going to reach that goal? No! But the boys loved that I tried, that I played. The call of "wounded warrior" still makes me laugh and run as I know a very large Woodbury boy is about to scoop me up, throw me over his shoulder, and run through the house as they laugh and I scream. Making crazy, fun memories together lets our children know that life as a family, a Christian family, is meant to be lived in joy! On Ben's first Christmas home from college, we were playing or doing some- thing fun together when he disclosed, "I like that you do this with me, Mom. I can't see any of my friends at college having fun like this with their mom."

Wherever we have lived or traveled, our family of four established a precedent that fun was accepted and expected! Times of family togetherness are fewer now as the boys have gone off to college and usually have different spring breaks. So when the time arose for us to drive Ben in his pickup truck to college in South Carolina from Clovis, New Mexico, I was thrilled about the family adventure. We packed up everything Ben needed for college in the back of his truck. With no way to secure the belongings at night, at each hotel, we hauled in three large car-top carriers—which looked like full body bags—to endless grumbles, uproarious laughter, and great embarrassment. From state to state we sang, we laughed, we ate, we ate, we ate; and after that experience, we made the same trip two more times! In the cramped truck, the joy was priceless!

We have found that "a cheerful heart is good medicine" (Prov. 17:22). Our family many times has had to choose joy. If I am down, Matt has learned to pull out his "dinosaur" jump for a good laugh. It's nothing I can explain on paper, but my six-foot-five, two-hundred-forty-pound son jumping up with arms held close like a T-rex and squawking like a dinosaur always makes me smile. There will be times in your family, as in ours, that fun was not appropriate for the day, but joy had to be. So we chose, "This is the day the Lord has made. Let us rejoice and be glad in it." I don't know where I learned this song, but I chose to sing it many times. "Praise the Lord, Allelu, I don't care what the devil's goanna do. His word and faith are my sword and shield. Jesus is the Lord of the way I feel."

We have all experienced when a song gets stuck in our head, and we hum or sing it all day. Family fun and laughter, even with sometimes deliberate humiliation, is something I want stuck in my boys' heads. Choosing joy may not be letting loose on a rendition of "Country Roads" or belting out tunes in the shower, but the freedom to laugh and be crazy with family is something that will be embedded in our children's memories and will give rise to their desire to choose joy! After all, they may want to have a fun home like yours one day!

Punishment or Reeewards

Snack time after school was filled with either fun stories of hilarious antics of the day, or it was filled with a sudden, alarming dread that resulted in physical or emotional affliction—in other words, stress! You guessed it. The boys coming home from school either meant punishment or reward, both for them and for me! One particular afternoon when Matt was a freshman in high school, I was given an extraordinary reward. Nonchalantly while consuming his snack, Matt affirmed, "Mom, thanks for raising me the way you did." Wow, we could have stopped there for me to have all the reward I required, but then he expounded, "Because I say 'Yes, ma'am' and 'Thank you,' all the teachers like me. And then they tell my coaches!" It seemed that Matt was at least beginning to understand the rewards one got for having manners.

When I grew up, manners, or politely speaking to people with graciousness, was not an option. I was taught to say "Yes, ma'am" or "No, ma'am" to adults and to always say please and thank you. Some people, as I have noticed recently, have moved away from this practice, believing it to be just an old Southern tradition. Yet I believe it is a Christian principle. To respect authority, to let your words be seasoned with grace, and to honor others are not theories made up by a Southern grandma, but are foundations given by God's words. Our words of thankfulness stream from the content of our hearts. Learning to say thank you to people at any early age, teaches children a biblical lesson that instructs them to be thankful in every circumstance and to give thanks always (1 Thess. 5:18, Eph. 5:20). Some of the most special times in our parenting were when we heard the boys voice gratitude to God, to us, or to someone else. We cherished the small voice we heard from a three-year-old, "Zank you for mama, daddy, Barney, and Michael Jordan." (He loved the movie Space Jam.) After the first t-ball practice, one of them voiced, "Jesus, thank you for giving my bat the strength to hit far and high." Our hearts delighted in Ben's declaration: "Thank you, Jesus, for reminding me to ask you into my heart."

As I had learned manners and the importance of showing thanks and gratitude, I taught my boys the same valuable codes of behavior and expression born from knowing and experiencing God's character. People have even tried to get my boys not to say, "Yes, sir." Their response to that was, "Yes, sir." I actually was told by a coach that he had been "yes, sir-ed to death" by Matt. I guess that would be a pleasant way to go. It seems that Ben and Matt understood the reward portion of using good manners, but often times, to instill the trait even more, they also had to receive the punishment portion. When the boys were unwilling to choose not to speak with graciousness or use manners, one consequence they sometimes received was to read a book I had called, *A Little Book of Manners for Boys*. It's amazing how just the mention of having to read a book like that led to much nicer behavior.

As middle school boys, one of their favorite movies was *Holes*. The movie was about a group of juvenile offenders sent to a work camp. The young lawbreakers were told by the two comical wardens of the camp that in order to build character, they were to dig holes in the desert every day, all day. With a thick Southern accent, Mr. Sir, played by Jon Voight, articulated over and over to the boys the choice they had before them, "Punishment or Reeeward." Well, it turned out that the wardens of the detention camp were imposters, having the boys dig for lost treasure from a legend told long ago. But the tenet of these two fake characters had merit: we get to choose "Punishment or Reeeward."

Sometimes children try to manipulate punishment or reward to suit their interest while not understanding the bigger concept being taught. Strolling through the mall one day, Ben came upon a phenomenal invention—the massage chair. As he sat there enjoying the massage, he concluded, "I know we should get this for a time out chair!" Unlike Ben, who tried to blur the lines between punishment and rewards, the Bible makes plain the punishments and rewards of God for his children. Second Samuel 7:14 declares, "I will be his father and he will be my son. When he does wrong, I will punish him with the rod of men, with floggings inflicted by men." On the other hand, Jeremiah 17:9–10 points out, "The heart is deceitful above all things and beyond cure. Who can understand it? I the Lord search the heart and examine the mind, to reward each person according to their conduct, according to what their deeds deserve." The overarching character of God in both the punishment and reward of his children is stated in 2 Samuel 7:15, "But my love will never be taken away from them." God convicts out of His kindness and creates boundaries out of His wisdom. God punishes and rewards out of love for His children.

God clearly lays out His expectations for His children and then asks them to choose. "If you are willing and obedient, you will see the best from the land. But if you resist and rebel, you will be devoured by the sword" (Isa. 1:19–20). "See, I set before you today life and prosperity, death and destruction. For I command you today to love the Lord your God, to walk in his ways, and to keep his commands, decrees and laws: that you will live and increase and the Lord your God will bless you in the land you are entering to possess. But, if your heart turns away and you are not obedient, and if you are drawn away to bow down to other gods and worship them, I declare to you this day that you will certainly be destroyed. You will not live long in the land you are crossing the Jordan to enter and possess. This day I call heaven and earth as witnesses against you that I have set before you life and death, blessings and curses, Now choose life so that you and your children may live." (Deut. 30:15–20) It seemed that Joshua understood God's parenting style. God laid out the options and the consequences of those options clearly—choosing the Lord brings life, and choosing other gods brings death. So Joshua then proclaimed his choice boldly, "As for me and my household we will serve the Lord" (Josh. 24:15b).

During a Vacation Bible School lesson when Ben was almost five years old, the teacher was reading the story of the woman at the well. The book continued to report that the woman was bad.

Ben sat quietly through the lesson, listening and discerning what he had heard. When the review time came, he quickly raised his hand in objection, "Miss Glee, that lady was not bad. She just made bad choices." The boys learned as we set out clear expectations and the consequences of each choice that the power resided in their hands to make choices—good or bad. An illustration I used in helping my boys understand this concept came from the book, *Shepherding a Child's Heart* by Tedd Tripp. On a piece of paper, a circle is drawn with a figure in it. This represents the child inside the boundaries set by godly parents. While inside the circle, the child has chosen obedience to the rules and expectations laid out by the parents and thus, enjoys safety, protection, and good rewards. If the child steps out of the boundaries of the circle and disobeys the rules and expectations set forth by the parents, then punishments or negative consequences are the result of their choosing to step out of safety into danger or peril. This picture, which is so easily understood even by a small child, enabled Ben and Matt to understand they had the choice to receive punishment or reward. By using this method, I was also able to separate myself from the idea that I had punished them but realized they had chosen the punishment. I would sometimes ask them, "Now by choosing this behavior, you are telling me that you WANT the punishment?"

"Thank you for letting me stand up for what is right," Ben prayed as a four-year-old. How did he, as such a young child, even know what is right and what is wrong? From the earliest times in his life, we taught, we set boundaries, we shared from God's word behaviors that God rewards and punishes, and he was able to form his concept of what is right and be thankful. Sometimes as adults, the same choices and options are set before us to either be rewarded in some way or receive a type of punishment. Matt was always larger than his peers. When provoked, Matt could display quite a temper for a very young child; and because of his size, that was a bit scary at times. During his time in kindergarten, he was learning that restraint brought reward and lack thereof brought punishment. He had shown tremendous restraint when a smaller yet slightly older child in the neighborhood continued to bully Matt. The child had spit on Matt on the playground, had slapped his face while at a birthday party, and had continued similar behaviors in different venues without Matt lifting a hand back to him. I was extremely proud of Matt and livid at the same time, so I decided that it was time to talk with his mother and to present her with choices that would accompany various consequences. After I explained to the mother what had been going on, she was unmoved by her child's unruly behavior, so I presented these two options. First, she could take charge of her child and discipline him so he would not bully Matt again. Or I would allow Matt to take care of the situation next time it occurred. Set before her two options, she chose wisely. Matt was not bothered by this child again.

The first time Ben really noticed or responded to beggars or homeless people was in Jerusalem as we were touring the old city. The city was packed, and we had to hold on to each other closely to not lose one another. People were bumping into us, vendors were yelling, and crippled people were begging. Ben innocently turned to us with a question, "Mom, doesn't he know begging won't get him anywhere?" Now that's what Ben knew; that's what he was taught. But the question Ben asked was important: "Doesn't he know?" Ben wanted to know if that beggar didn't' get the information so that he could choose the right thing. Our obligation as parents is to let our children know, clearly and consistently, so they can choose punishment or reeeward.

A trip to Baskin Robbins with their dad would surely be a treat for any boy, but without knowing, Ben was being taken to get ice cream and to have a serious "talk" with his dad about girls! With the ice cream piled high with all the fixings, Ben dug in to this amazing treat he had been waiting for. No sooner had he begun eating when Greg began his discussion right there in the ice cream store. Ben, listening to every word, slowed his eating and eventually pushed his ice cream away. Stating that he felt a bit queasy, Ben was ready to rush out of the situation with the hope that Dad would stop talking. When returning home to his younger brother Matt, he offered some very important advice about choices: "If Dad ever asks you to go to Baskin Robbins alone, just say NO!"

No More "John Wayne" Words

When the boys were little babies, I would put my lips on their sweet fat cheeks and voice words very slowly and carefully so they could begin to learn to voice words to talk. Like all other parents, we proudly wrote down each new word, and even if it was indecipherable, we chose to believe that our child was talking brilliantly. As they listened to us, they learned to speak. So there was no surprise when my toddler Ben greeted everyone he met with a Southern, "Hey, darlin'."

As they grew in their abilities, new teaching opportunities arose. We realized that teaching the boys to talk meant more than just teaching them to form words, but it meant teaching them the meaning of words, when to use them, and with what tone to use them. Ultimately, this teaching also took the form of teaching them what NOT to say.

One weekend, at a family gathering at my mom and dad's house, my appalled nephew ran into the house yelling, "Aunt Kathy, Aunt Kathy, Ben cussed at me!" Because we are from a family that never cusses, I immediately ran to my four-year-old Ben to determine what in the world could have caused this breakdown in the family values. I calmly asked him what he had said to Jeremy. With hands on his hips and with a distinct cowboy swagger, Ben lowered his voice as much as a preschool boy could and drawled these words that he had spoken to his cousin, "Get the hell outta here!" Trying not to act overly shocked or dismayed while being quite amused because I already knew the culprit, I questioned Ben about where he had heard those words. His answer, "John Wayne says it all the time." With my dad's largest hero now in the hot seat, this was our first lesson on the words we hear that ought not to be repeated. Therefore our first word ban was enacted—all John Wayne words.

So began our extensive teaching on words, the hearing of the words that others use, and the choosing of the words that we use. Why would some words be okay and some not? Who deems which words are acceptable? Why do the same words sound different when saying them with different tones? Why do words have the same meaning sometimes and different meanings other times? We say words flippantly as adults when we understand the meaning, but children must be taught. We were having a discussion about food one day when I explained to Ben that the bacon and ham we eat is pig and that the roast Grandma serves for Sunday dinner is cow. Days later, I didn't understand why he refused one of his favorite menu items—a hotDOG! Together, as parent and child, we persisted in our attempt to learn how to talk and to listen.

As the boys heard more and more words from outside our home, more and more discussions crept in; and yes, more words were banned. The "s" word was definitely unauthorized. So when our preacher during a Sunday sermon continued to use THE WORD, Ben became agitated and extremely provoked in the pew as if God himself were being assaulted. After the sermon, before the last note of the final hymn was sung, Ben righteously marched his kindergarten self straight to the preacher and defiantly exclaimed, "You are never to tell Jesus to SHUT UP!" The essence of the sermon had been how we are sometimes "shut up to Jesus." The next Sunday night, when the second half of the series was presented, little listening ears approved as the sermon title became, "Closed Off to Jesus."

What a process! First, we teach our children to voice the sounds that make words, then we teach them to learn the meaning that the words create when joined together, then we teach them to discern what should or should not be said. Sometimes, in all our teaching of words, we forget that they are hearing not only our words but the tone in which we speak. Then we get a lesson—the hard way—and we become the student, the one learning to talk. This lesson came harshly for me when Ben was in the first or second grade. Sitting in the car having a discussion on a topic Ben certainly did not like at the time, he spewed out three words that literally pierced my heart: "I hate you!" Those words coming from my baby held so much power that I felt that I had failed forever as a mom and that I would never recover. How could he say that? Did he really feel that? Where did he get the venom spewing from his tongue?

A wave of conviction came as quickly as I had thought through those questions, and I knew the answers. Those particular words have never been voiced in our home; but sometimes harsh tones, sarcastic words, hurtful or unkind speech are used when we forget to choose our words, and we forget that little people are hearing and are learning how to talk from me. I went home, got out my Bible, and began to look up and record every verse that had the word mouth or tongue in it. God had to teach me to talk! God's grace is so good. He forgives, and He covers my parenting mistakes over and over. So as a teacher to my boys, I allowed these verses through the power of the Holy Spirit to teach me over and over. "May the words of my mouth and the meditation of my heart be pleasing in your sight, O Lord My Rock and my redeemer" (Ps. 19:14). I had a visual in Psalm 141:3: "Set a guard over my mouth, O Lord Keep watch over the door of my lips." I kept this picture of God guarding my words as I again began teaching Ben to talk but now with renewed understanding of my words as teacher. I considered using duct tape over my mouth to help me with my new adventure in guarding my words, but Job 29:9 offered a more politically correct directive, "The chief men restrained from speaking and covered their mouth with their hands." Psalm 17:3 now had to be my prayer, "Though you probe my heart and examine me at night, though you test me, you will find nothing: I have resolved that my mouth will not sin." I prayed for Ben, asked his forgiveness, and then together we again persevered in the journey that is learning to talk.

Words have power, and it matters what we say. Our Turkish friend who helped us many times as our tour guide in Turkey was very close to Matt. She was astonished that a preschool child would desire to sit with her and just chat with an adult. But one day, with no filter and completely innocent, Matt told our friend that she was going to die. Shocked by such a brazen announcement, she asked

Matt why he thought that. With the honesty of a child, he replied, "Because you are fat and you smoke." Quickly, I did the prudent and adult thing and required Matt to apologize. Our friend just smiled yet held on to those very authentic words from a child. Years later, our friend who still lives in Turkey asked Greg to tell Matt that she had never forgotten his words as a small child. She quit smoking, and she lost weight and is very healthy.

I was not prepared for the preteen years followed by the teen years. I had no idea that at this point in parenting, I would be the student of language, and different languages at that. The boys had somehow mastered a whole set of nonverbal skills—the rolling of the eyes, the shrug of the shoulders, and the endless sigh before I had even known they had acquired them. Along with these highly intelligible nonverbal communications were also materializing strange verbal expressions of "whatever" the teen years taught them. Being the ever-mindful mom, I learned that in order to teach them to talk, I also needed to learn. Not only did I need to listen to their words, but I had to decipher what in the world these words meant! I love the statement that I have heard passed down for years that God gave us two ears and one mouth for a reason. Listening was the only way I was going to go beyond these words to actually hear what my boys were saying. Proverbs 18:13 says it best, "He who answers before listening—that is his folly and shame." I did not want to go there again. So I listened, and I learned.

I discovered that "sick," "nasty," and "bad," when voiced by a teenage boy, were not negative terms but positive descriptors. I learned that "sweet" does not describe a tasty dessert but an affirmation of something with which the boys agree. I also identified that "smooth" is not a word about texture, but about the sound of something. I ascertained upon much repetition that when Matt used the term "pretty much," that meant he really had no idea what he was talking about. In my adult mind one spring, I was attempting to converse with Matt, then sixteen, about how thankful I was that God gave us seasons so we wouldn't be bored. Matt agreed with a, "Yeah, like baseball season." When the boys were babies, I had to listen carefully to the words they formed and what it meant to them. So I just applied the same logic when they were teenagers. I attempted to learn their gibberish and did as James 1:19 admonishes, "Be slow to speak and quick to listen."

I recall stating quite piously many years ago that I would never carry a phone in my pocketbook. That seemed ridiculous. After all, what would be so important that I would need to have a phone in the grocery store or at a friend's house or at church? Now I had teenage boys, and I praised the Lord for Verizon! I still can't understand how my parents could have let me go to college and not be able to communicate with me except for my dorm room rotary-dial phone. That did cause some difficulty for my parents, and consequently for me, in 1981. But the cell phone has also created a new dilemma for talking and listening to my boys today. When they were very young, I became painfully aware that the boys picked up on every inflection of my voice and determined my every motive based on their interpretation of the tone. We eventually learned what each other's tone usage meant and thus learned to communicate more effectively. But now, we are texting, and the inflection issue has again posed quit a predicament. Ben, who can be quite sensitive to every intonation, can pickup on a feeling of mine just by a word or lack thereof, and heaven forbid if I forget to include a smiley face at the end of a line. And of course, yelling with all caps is still a parental prerogative as well as including many exclamation marks!!!! In order to have significant discourse, we persevere to learn this new language. This education will probably continue until technology is improved, and we move to something else. Whatever comes, from infants to teen, from verbal words to texts, this journey of learning to talk and listen to our children will continue.

When Ben was two years old, we were looking around a pet store in a mall when from nowhere, a rude parrot chimed into our conversation, looked at Ben, and exclaimed, "You don't talk so good." Being the protective mom that I am, I instinctively began defending my precious son to a bird! "He is only two years old," I quipped. Then I looked around to see other patrons watching me argue with a bird about my son's communication skills. After all, who was a parrot to make such judgments about my son's speech?

Matt arrived from kindergarten one day after being schooled in phonetics, and promptly and quite candidly informed me that I did not pronounce his brother's name correctly. Taken aback by the audacity of my five-year-old, I informed him that although the correct pronunciation may be "Ben," with a short *e*, his brother would always be "Bin," with a short *i* sound, to me. I am from South Carolina! Now I had a bird and a five-year-old boy making judgments about how communication should occur. But as I had to teach the boys, there IS someone who perfectly judges our speech. If we take away the John Wayne words, and we get rid of the "s" words, there must be something to replace them. Therefore, I taught them from the Word to discover what the Judge of All teaches us about what to speak and how to speak. "Do not let any unwholesome talk come out of your mouths, but only what is helpful for building others up according to their needs that it will benefit those who listen" (Eph. 4:29) "Let your conversation be always full of grace, seasoned with salt, so that you may know how to answer everyone" (Col. 4:6). "Nor should there be obscenity, foolish talk, or course joking which are out of place, but rather thanksgiving" (Eph. 5:4).

We sang a song when the boys were young: "Be careful, little ears, what you hear. Be careful, little ears, what you hear, for the Father up above is looking down in love. So be careful, little ears, what you hear." Ben liked the *Little Rascals* application for this. When he didn't want to hear something, he put his little hands over his ears and chanted, "I'm not hearing this. I'm not hearing this." Ben chose what he wanted to hear. The song continues with, "Be careful, little mouth, what you say." We choose what we want to say and how we say it. The importance of teaching our children how to voice words far exceeds the sweetness and importance of their first word. Our teaching them to listen and to speak provides the framework for them to listen and speak to God. If they know we hear them and understand the words they say, they may believe God will hear them even more. As they learn to put meaning to their words, they may communicate with the parent far greater than us. "Because he turned his ear to me, I will call on him as long as I live" (Ps. 116:2).

Green Grass in the Desert

Upon hearing that we would be moving to Albuquerque, New Mexico, for our next duty station, I immediately began praying for a house we could call home. I knew nothing about Albuquerque, except for the cartoon suggesting that Bugs Bunny take a left turn there. Louisville, Kentucky, was as far west as I had ever been or lived in the States, so I had no expectations for our new home. Moving in the military is just part of the agreement, and with our family, so is lots of prayer for each move. Each move brings many considerations. Should we live on or off base? Where are the best schools for the boys? Do we rent or buy? If we live off base, how far is the commute? Is the neighborhood safe when Greg deploys? What are the expenses? Then the really important question: will our California king bed fit in the master bedroom? These are the usual questions, but I never considered the dilemma that might be encountered when a girl from South Carolina moves to New Mexico.

My first- and third-grade boys were very active and mostly played outside where they could hit, throw, kick, or punch a ball. So one of my priority prayers was a big-enough yard to accommodate their fun! I wanted grass, and I had no idea that I was asking for a miracle. We left Turkey, where we were currently stationed, and visited family in South Carolina before making our trek out west. After our visit, we loaded up the minivan and headed cross-country for our new adventure. As we made our way through North Carolina, Tennessee, Oklahoma, Texas, and eventually, New Mexico, the trees became smaller and quite different, the sky became much bigger, and the green grass turned to brown rocks. Upon entering Albuquerque, Ben commented sheepishly, "Mom, this looks like Turkey."

The very next day, our house hunt began. We immediately found answers to our usual moving questions: yes, we would rent, not buy. Yes, we chose an area in the city with great schools. And for that reason, no, we would not live on base. I am always so excited about looking at houses at our new assignments and making each house our home, and this was no exception. We had given the realtor the list of expectations, the first being a big yard for the boys. After seeing the first house, it was clear to me that she did not understand what I had said. The yard, as she called it, was nothing more than a rock garden with a patch of grass! I restated clearly our need, and after feeling that our realtor finally valued our desires, we forged on to look at more houses. With great promise, the inside of the next house was perfect, then we opened the backdoor to what? Did I not see the yard? What in the world was going on? After all, I was not asking for an acre of land with plush green grass, just a place for my boys to play ball! Certainly, the realtor could not be that ill advised. Her job was to listen to the desires of her clients. Then the truth fell hard like a weighted brick when she politely tried to enlighten me on property in Albuquerque. "This," she said, "IS a lot of grass. I don't think you will find better in this town. Welcome to the desert." But she didn't know that we had prayed in advance for a yard; we had prayed for grass!

Trying not to lose hope, Greg and I found a listing for a rental house on the bulletin board on base and decided to quickly go see the house while the family was moving out. I was not concerned about the condition of the house. I ran past moving boxes, trash, junked up counters, and stunned renters as I darted to the back yard and saw our promised land. There was an underground swimming pool, a cement basketball court, and enough green grass for a family of four with two little boys to play and to run and to live!

God has given us grass in the desert many times. He promises in 1 Corinthians 2:9, "No eye has seen, no ear has heard, no mind has conceived what God has prepared for those who love him." The reason God gives good gifts is that God is good. My oldest son recently suggested to me that people use the word "good" too often. We say the movie was good, the pizza was good, the grade was good, and the conversation was good. But all that "goodness" is relative. God's goodness is infinite, meaning it lasts forever; and God's goodness is immutable, meaning that it will never change; and God's goodness is perfect, meaning it is complete, not halfway. God IS good. That is who He is; therefore, He can be nothing other than His character. A. W. Tozer wrote that "God is kindhearted, gracious, good-natured, and benevolent in intention" (*The Attributes of God*, vol. 1). Psalm 119:68 says, "You are good and what you do is good."

At times, it is difficult for us to accept God's good gifts toward us. We somehow feel unworthy or undeserving. We are unworthy and undeserving. God gives us good gifts not because of who we are but because of who HE is. Psalm 100:5 says, "For the Lord is good and His love endures forever; his faithfulness continues through all generations." Pastors and their families understand that weekends are workdays, so a weekend off is a precious rarity that should be used wisely. Our first active duty station was at Moody Air Force Base in Valdosta, Georgia. Greg was the pastor of the Gospel service on base, so on one of those rare weekends when he didn't have to preach, we scheduled a trip to Orlando, Florida, to go to Disney World. The van was packed, the hotel reserved, and two over-zealous toddlers were fastened in the backseat raring to go. We had just left the city limits when a terrible sound and a huge clunk came from the undercarriage of the van. Neither Greg nor I are mechanically inclined, but we both recognized that was probably not a positive sound. We pulled into the nearest garage/tire shop. The mechanic looked at the van for what seemed like hours. The boys were restless, though still excited about the prospects of seeing Mickey, Pluto, and Donald Duck. As time passed, I grew fearful that our Disney trip would not happen, and our only weekend off would be spent waiting to get our car fixed. After many hours, the owner of the shop asked us to come into his office. That was it. I waited for the bad news. He said that he did not have the part to fix the car now, and it was too dangerous to drive the car. But he handed Greg a set of keys to a rental car that he had already paid for and said, "Take your family to Disney World this weekend. The car is on me." We didn't know this man at all, but he knew God. Greg tried not to accept this good gift, but the owner of the tire store replied, "You have to accept this gift from God, or you will be robbing me of the opportunity to participate in God's goodness." So we all four piled into what the boys thought was our new car and took off for Disney World. Through tears and bewilderment all the way to see Mickey, Greg and I "rejoiced in all the good things the Lord your God has given to you and your household" (Deut. 26:11).

We are often surprised by God's good gifts to us. We either don't know about the goodness of God, or we don't think to look for it. It is similar to Ben when he was a senior in high school. I told him that we should start collecting names to send out invitations to his graduation. He wondered why we would send these invitations to people who we knew wouldn't be able to attend; after all, we lived in Colorado and all of our family lived on the east coast. Knowing he didn't fully understand, I asked, "Don't you want graduation presents?" With renewed energy for the task, Ben inquired, "You mean I get gifts from people just because I graduate high school?" Ben didn't know about the gifts, but scripture informs us about God's gifts. "O Sovereign Lord, you are God! Your words are trustworthy, and you have promised these good things to your servant" (2 Sam. 7:28).

After living in Turkey for a year, we decided to take a hop to Italy. That means a military plane was leaving Turkey headed for Italy, and if there was space available for passengers on leave, then you can catch a ride. Well, there was space for the four of us, so we hopped aboard! Our neighbor in Turkey was Italian and graciously offered us her apartment in Aviano as a launching point for our Italian vacation. She also graciously offered to have her cousin, who spoke no English, pick us up from the Air Force Base that we flew into. We arrived in the dark of night and were greeted by her cousin who drove us to the apartment and dropped us off. After a long day, we all went straight to bed. In the morning, we were awakened by a refreshing gift from God. Church bells were ringing! The boys, who for a year had heard only the calls of the Muslim Imam five times a day, ran to the window to find a large church with people walking in the open doors. The boys screamed with excitement, "Hey, look, people in this country go to church." We sat listening to the bells and watching the people enter the church, and I thought, what a good and perfect gift of refreshment we needed yet did not realize. Psalm 107:9 declares, "For he satisfies the thirsty and fills the hungry with good things."

We know that "every good and perfect gift is from above, coming down from the Father of the heavenly lights, who does not change like shifting shadows" (James 1:17). What a fun opportunity we have as parents to give good gifts to our children! While doing so, we teach them about the ultimate giver of all good gifts.

When Matt was young, he absolutely loved balloons, especially blue balloons. Matt had memorized his AWANA scriptures, secured his bucks, and now it was the all-important night—AWANA store night where the children get to trade their bucks in for prizes. Matt was delighted to show us his purchase of a great big blue helium balloon. Unfortunately, just as quickly as he proudly exhibited his balloon, it was snatched out of his hands by another child, and we watched as Matt's big blue helium balloon wafted slowly to the top of the gym ceiling. Matt was devastated and my heart sank! We tried to console him, but no words were good enough as he looked at the balloon he purchased with his own hard work was now so far out of reach. The next day, I was determined to show Matt the overwhelming goodness of God in the midst of what seemed like a horrible, insurmountable problem to a seven-year-old. All day, I worked. After school, Matt came home and opened the door to his bedroom where he was met by a sea of blue balloons covering his entire room—even more than he could ever thought or imagined. Now if I, as an earthly parent, would give good gifts to my child, how much more would our heavenly Father do for us (Matt. 7:11)?

Christmas time in a remote location can become quite hectic for parents who want to give the "good gifts" the children want. It seemed that the boys were totally clueless to the fact that we had ONE store (the Base Exchange) in which to get everything on their list—unless, of course, they disclosed their list in time for us to order it and have it shipped to Turkey. This Christmas was no different, and it was a bit late in the game when Ben put in his order for a purple Game Boy. How specific can one be? And what are the odds that a purple Game Boy would show up in the Base Exchange in Incirlik,

Turkey, just when we needed it? So with the words of Psalm 84:11 in mind, "The Lord bestows favor and honor; no good thing does he withhold from those whose walk is blameless," I trekked to the BX daily to see if that "Good Gift" would show up. Lo and behold, one day, it was there. There was only one problem. Someone else was holding it. From one aisle over, I watched—okay, stalked—the man holding the purple Game Boy. He carefully looked at it and then put it down. I continued to hide, not wanting him to see me in case he may think I wanted The Game Boy, understand its value, and keep it for himself. My strategy was failing, and my heart palpitating as he picked it up again. Still not seeing me, the man committed a fatal shopping error in Turkey. He put the Game Boy down again to contemplate his purchase. With that mistake, I rounded the corner with absolutely no reserve or decorum, snatched up the Game Boy, and ran to the checkout counter! All the while I praised the Lord for His good gift and decided that I was just following the Proverb which tells us, "Do not withhold good from those who deserve it, when it is in your power to act"(Prov. 3:27). I'm not sure stalking other customers in a store to get a gift for my son was the meaning behind the scripture, but I do know that as our children see us go above and beyond to give good gifts to them. They may understand even more how God, who is eternally good, will go above and beyond to give good gifts to them.

Good gifts from God look different every day. One day, it may be a nighttime hug from a toddler who has worn you out during the day; or a random, "Mama, thanks for the boundaries. I know it means you love me," from a teenage boy; or another parent who arbitrarily comments on how wonderful your sons are; or an unexpected text from a college son that says, "I love you with all my heart, Mom." A good gift was given to me one day after a big tribulation. Matt was able to say, "This is not God's punishment. It is God's good." Not every gift looks good to us at the moment, but as we *know* that God is *good*, we can *trust* that His Gift is *good*. It was not good that Ben left one college not knowing what he would do, but it was good that at that time, he was able to be at home while Greg was deployed. It was not good that Greg did not get an assignment that he had always wanted, but it was good that we got to stay close to Matt's college for another year of his growing. Many things have not seemed good, but we have remembered who is good. "I will tell of the kindnesses of the Lord, the deeds for which he is to be praised, according to all the Lord has done for us. Yes, the many good things he has done for the house of Israel according to his compassion and many kindnesses" (Isa. 63:7).

When the boys were very young, if they enjoyed something we were doing, they would hold out their hands; and with simple yet trusting words, beg, "Do 'gin." As I have tasted and seen that the Lord is good, I want to plead with Him in simple yet trusting words, "Do 'gin."

Just Follow the Tour Guide

"No problem, *abla*," the Turkish man said calmly as he grabbed Ben and began carrying him like a football up a very steep mountain. I was running behind shouting, and Greg was bringing up the rear-dragging Matt as we all tried to forge ahead to keep up with our zealous guide. The man disregarded my broken Turkish and evidently did not understand the English word "stop" or the phrase, "Yes, I have a problem." He had my son and was climbing the mountain faster than I could think of my next move, so I continued yelling in panic and continued climbing.

For months, we had been locked down on the base in Turkey, unable to go anywhere because of problems with terrorists in the country. So as soon as the Office of Special Investigations (OSI) gave the green light to leave the base, we took off to the nearest sightseeing adventure. It was the closest adventure to base, and it was the first adventure of many we would take together as a military family.

Because we were so new to oversees adventures and so eager to go somewhere, out of our naivety, we did not adequately plan for our first outing. We did not go with a group, nor did we seek out a guide who could help us with our trip; therefore, we were left with a Turkish bystander who took it upon himself to be our guide in a way in which I definitely did not approve. So all the way up to Snake Castle, we raced behind a Turkish man with Ben on his back, Greg dragging Matt, and me yelling, "Evet, problem," which in Turkish means, "YES, problem." By the time we finally reached the man and Ben, it was too late to turn back. We were committed to the adventure. The Turkish man who had brought us part of the way was nowhere to be found when the climb really got rough, and we all were on hands and knees crawling between ledges with huge drops on both sides. Thankfully, God looked out for us in our ignorance and sent several single airmen who were also sightseeing on Snake Castle that day, who eagerly helped us maneuver the ruins with our two young boys, who by the way were having a blast. Obviously, we made it down from the ruins and back to base, where later, there was a warning given about venturing out to Snake Castle: "Keep in mind safety and protection measures on the castle is the responsibility of the visitor. Climbing up and walking around the castle ruins is very difficult, and one should watch their own footing and also always keep very close watch on small children." And why was it called Snake Castle?

A guide is one who goes ahead, who leads, who knows the way. A guide has already been where they are taking you. A guide is one who assists through travels to help reach the destination. A guide is familiar with the way where we are not familiar. Through our many adventures, I have learned much about guides. On Snake Castle, I learned that you better get one! Don't just let a stray person take over that role. They may not do what you want because you don't speak the same language. Also, I better have a guide I can trust to take me the whole journey and not abandon me when it gets rough.

After our first, very haphazard adventure in Turkey, we decided to secure a very reliable guide. She became our friend as well as our guide for many trips. She came to know us and thus, knew what we would like. She arranged many wonderful and successful trips to Ephesus, Cappadocia, Cyprus, Israel, Greece, and more. Each time, I trusted her more and more as the trips far exceeded my expectations. But I had overheard some friends talking about a trip they had taken, and I became restless to go on that trip. I approached our guide about taking the Turkish train to Ankara as my friends had done. After all, it only cost forty dollars for a family of four for the weekend train trip—on a sleeper car! My friends had a great time, and surely, my tour guide would book it for me immediately. When I inquired about the weekend train trip to Ankara, my guide gently began advising me against it, and in her sweet Turkish accent pleaded, "Katy, I know you. You would not like it." Feeling somewhat slighted and determined to have my own way regardless of the knowledgeable and wise guidance I was given, I talked her into booking the trip. She reluctantly made the plans and prearranged that she would meet us at the train station to see us off.

Resolved to prove to my guide that I was up for this rustic and antiquated type of adventure, I put on a happy face, said good-bye, and loaded our little clan on the train. We walked through a gauntlet of Turkish men smoking throughout the train as we attempted to locate our little sleeper car. Before entering our individual car, another train passed by that I couldn't help noticing. People with drab clothing and sullen faces were stuffed in the train. I suddenly felt as if I were witnessing a scene from a World War II movie. Then it dawned on me that I was on a similar train with similar people. Before the train pulled out, we found our car with two bunk beds up against the walls and a small table by the window. *What an adventure! I can do this,* I thought. After all, the boys were having a great time, the Turkish men were teaching them card tricks, and we played and laughed the entire way to Ankara.

What in the world was our guide worried about? The trip to Ankara, although a bit rough, was exciting. When we arrived in Ankara, we jumped in one of the thousand taxies at our disposal; and with a picture of TGI Fridays in hand, we conquered Ankara all while eating good American food. The weekend was over, and I was prepared to gloat to my guide about my ability to tackle with grace any situation Turkey could throw at me; but then we got on the train at night. The ride home was exceedingly different. A terrible thunderstorm began as we pulled out of the station. The boys were exhausted, so they fell fast asleep quickly. Then it began, the NIGHT train ride. The tunnels we rode through in the day became pitch black darkness at night, and the sounds of the rickety 1920 tracks and the screeches of the old train mixed with the thundering, lighting, and rain became a frightening musical that kept my heart pounding and my eyes wide open. I lay quietly on my bunk, sure that as the train went around another sharp curve, it would jump the tracks, and we would all die from a terrible crash. So in my heart, I prayed and began to sing hymns in my mind. Wanting to see if I were the only chicken in the group, I whispered to Greg to ask if he were awake. I asked if he thought we ought to pray, and when he said, "Already been doing it!" my greatest fears were realized. She—my guide—was right. I didn't like this. For the remainder of the trip while the boys slept, Greg and I sang hymns quietly, praying we would make it home for another adventure.

Without much enthusiasm, I had to go back and report that her guidance was good, and I should know that she had my best in her mind when she made suggestions. From that bold trip to Ankara, I learned that it would serve me well to listen and heed the advice given by a loving guide. From that time on, when I made suggestions of places that I had heard of and my guide steered me away due to her knowledge of me or the place, I listened. Except when we ended up there by accident, like when we went to Konya, a place she told us never to go.

My parents came to visit for a month, so we turned to my guide once again. She mapped out a huge trip driving across Turkey, along the Mediterranean Sea, stopping at all the Seven Churches of Asia Minor. The trip was wonderful. She had booked a hotel for each night, each one more beautiful than the next. But the last night of our trip, she had directed us to the place, but had not made reservations saying they were not necessary in this small secluded lake town on our way back home. After a long day of travel and getting lost in Turkey without GPS, we finally arrived at the place our guide had so fondly spoken of as a place she loved so much that she wanted to be buried there. At first glance, I was skeptical about this being the correct hotel, so Greg and I went in the hotel first before hauling Mama, Daddy, Ben, and Matt out of the van. The attendant at the desk did not speak English, but he knew we desired to see a room. We entered a very old, very, very small elevator that immediately gave me the creeps. The hallway on the second floor was only partially lit, and the room he showed us had bare mattresses with previously used linens on the floor. The bathroom was Turkish style, which meant the shower and the toilet were the same thing, and it covered the whole bathroom. I knew in an instant that I, like my guide, would have to be buried here if I had to stay in this sinister old hotel; and with that, we veered from the plan of our guide and left!

She, after all, was only human, and her guidance on that particular day leaned more toward her preferences than the preference of the one she was guiding. She was not perfect, but we would have to pay the consequences for choosing to stray from our guide and that we did. We had no map, we had no GPS, and we had no idea where we were going to find a hotel. There was none in that small town. It was late at night, but we took off somewhere, anywhere. We saw lights up ahead and thought maybe it was a big beautiful hotel, so Greg pulled up to the gate. Armed Turkish police came up to the car. Frantically, Greg jumped out of the car, and in his haste, began asking questions in Spanish? The guards, not fooled, looked quizzically, smiled, and asked, "You American?" We learned that the beautiful building was a headquarters building for the Turkish Jandarma (Turkish military police), so they sent us on our way, and in a direction that led over a mountain on a very dark night. With all of us tired and sleepy, we began singing hymns and songs loudly so we could stay awake. We arrived finally in a big city—Konya. We recognized this as one of the towns that our guide said she would never book for Americans due to the fundamentalist Muslim population, but we were there. And God was there to take care of us and to guide us to safety, in the form of a Turkish policeman. Since we were the only people on the street at two in the morning, and we were in a Green Pontiac Montana, we did not exactly blend in with the population; so the policeman readily spotted us in our distress. He became our guide and escorted us to a Western-style hotel. Without our knowledge, he watched our car all night; and the next morning, he safely escorted us out of the city in the direction of home.

Once again, I learned much about guides, both positive and negative. I learned that human guides are not always perfect, and that if you stray from the path of guidance, you will have to pay the consequences. I enjoyed the trips where the guides told us when to get up, when to eat, when to shop, and when to be back at the bus and strictly enforced it. Our trips to Israel and Greece were much like that. Our tour guide in Israel wore a bright orange hat so we could see him as he went ahead of us, and as he waved his bright orange hat in the air, we would know to look at him for teaching or instruction.

The only problem was that he made all of us, the whole group, wear the same bright orange hat. It was a baseball cap, and it certainly did not go with every outfit I had prepared. For the sake of the group experience, I donned my lovely headgear each morning and followed my guide. I learned that it feels good to be a part of a larger group of same-hat-wearing people and follow a guide who is willing to look silly for the sake of leading.

All this touring about with guides has taught me valuable lessons about raising Ben and Matt. Two things I have learned: I have a Guide, and I am a Guide. I absolutely love the truth illustrated in Exodus 13:21, "By day the Lord went ahead of them in a pillar of cloud to guide them on their way and by night in a pillar of fire to give them light so they could travel by day or night." Now that is a guide with more than an orange hat! This is a guide who knows us better than we know ourselves, so His guidance is best. This is a guide who sees the road ahead and has already traveled it, so His guidance is trustworthy. This is a guide who will never abandon us and leave us unattended, so His guidance is always available. This is a guide whose information and word is perfect, so His guidance is always true. This is a guide who knows the plans He has for us, so His guidance will never lead us astray. Scripture promises us this guide. "He guides the humble in what is right and teaches them his way" (Ps. 25:9). "For this God is our God forever and ever, he will be our guide even to the end" (Ps. 48:14). "I guide you in the way of wisdom and lead you along straight paths" (Prov. 4:11).

Guiding the boys along straight paths sometimes required a physical nudge. You would think that vacationing on the beaches of the Mediterranean Sea would be extremely relaxing just watching the gorgeous sea and beautiful sand, and it would be if that was all you were going to see. The boys were so ready to get out of the car and run with Papa down to the beach on our long trek around Turkey. Walking down to the beach, Greg and I noticed two distinct sides as we crossed over the path and finally made it to the beach. On one side of the beach were the Turkish women covered from head to toe with clothing, and on the other side of the beach were the European women who were covered with nothing and seemed to think this was a clothing-optional beach. We quickly surrounded the boys to nudge them toward the Turkish side. We guided their path, and they followed without question and without knowing the hazards of the other side. We can't teach them how to see, but when they were young, we helped them know where to look. I was just praying my dad would follow our lead.

God is my guide, and He has given me these children and expects me to guide them as He has modeled guidance to me; but I don't know if "tour guiding" was His plan for me. We took off for Italy on the Freedom Bird, a military charter plane that arrived and left Turkey every Saturday, for our own excursion with no other guide than a *Fodor's Exploring Italy* book in hand and my pretend expertise. After being encouraged by church bells ringing the first morning after our arrival at night, I mustered my courage to be the guide. We rented a car and drove around Northern Italy enjoying— or running from—the birds in St. Mark's square in Venice, wearing jester hats around the ruins in Verona, taking crazy pictures with the leaning tower of Pisa, and most of all eating lots of gelato. It didn't take this tour guide long to realize that the way to appease a bored group of six- and seven-year-old boys waiting in line to see old statues and paintings was ice cream! Ben and Matt were troopers even when I tried to give information about the art and the artists we were seeing. Being an art major in college, I thought I would be able to expound intelligently on the artists, so I explained in first-grade terms about Michelangelo. My tour quickly turned sour when Ben first saw the gigantic statue of David by Michelangelo, with no clothes, and exclaimed in disgust, "MOM, you said he was a Christian. Why did he make him with no clothes on?' My tour ended; we moved on. Who wants gelato?

The week was amazing, and except for a few hiccups, I thought I was a marvelous tour guide. We arrived in Aviano to catch the Freedom Bird back to Turkey, but there was a problem. Back in the States, someone had not written the correct airframe on the manifest, so the Turks would not allow the plane to enter the country that night. Greg scrambled and decided we would catch a hop to Germany since there were no more planes going to Turkey from Italy for another week. We told the boys we were not going home, but instead were going to Germany. Then the indicting question about my tour guide ability arose as they both shrugged and sullenly asked, "Do we have to see any more statues?"

I don't think God was imploring us to be expert tour guides for our children. Maybe He meant more guidance along the line of Isaiah 42:16, "I will lead the blind by the ways they have not known, along unfamiliar paths, I will guide them. I will turn darkness into light before them and make the rough places smooth." He gives us children who are blank slates, who are blind to the ways of living. We are put in their lives to guide them in ways they have not known, to lead them along unfamiliar paths, to go before them to turn rough places smooth.

There is a problem however. We, like our tour guides, are imperfect guides. The scripture acknowledges this obstacle in Isaiah 9:16, "Those who guide this people mislead them, and those who are guided are led astray." In Matthew 15:14, it says, "Leave them, they are blind guides. If a blind man leads a blind man both will fall into a pit." We don't intend to mislead our children or guide them wrongly, but sometimes we lead haphazardly or lead with our interest in mind, or sometimes we don't lead at all. We can only lead as far as we have gone. We can only teach what we have learned. We will make mistakes. Sometimes, they may guide us, and we will learn with them. But with the responsibility to lead that our guide has given us, we can rest in the knowledge that we will be led as we lead, and we will have our guide to help us guide.

Our van trip driving around Turkey with me and Greg, our two boys, and my mom and dad was such a memorable adventure. We had the van packed with snacks, packaged oatmeal, water, and goodies; as well as all our suitcases for ten days; and games and toys to keep five- and seven-year-olds occupied. Matt had become sick on the trip, and by the time we reached Izmir, Greg decided to call the United States contingent in that city to inquire about a doctor that could see Matt. They graciously assisted us with the name and location of a Turkish doctor that saw service personnel for them. The problem was that in this very large city, we could not find the hospital, but we saw two Turkish police on a street corner and stopped to ask for directions. Instead of them telling us where to go, they asked if they could get in the van with the six of us and all our belongings so they could guide us personally to the hospital. At first, we balked at their suggestion since we had nowhere for them to sit, of course, no seatbelts; and we had piles of stuff everywhere. We thought there was just no room, but the helpful and insistent policemen eventually wore down our resolve. They climbed in the car, sat on the floor, and effortlessly guided us to the correct hospital.

Our guide is not standing around just handing out directions, He is present and going with us as He guides. So grab your bright-orange hat along with me, take up the challenge, and intentionally and with your presence lead your children in the way they should go.

The Power of Clothes

It is a basic need. It protects us from the elements such as sun, wind, and rain. It communicates to others what we do, what we like, who we are, and where we are from. It gives us a sense of social acceptance and self-esteem. By changing it, we are able to create different feelings and moods. Changing it also aids us in excelling in different enterprises. What is it that holds all this power? CLOTHES.

Clothes not only have great power over an individual, but also they have great power within a family system. They can either bring a family together with uproarious laughter or divide a family with great dissension. Our family has experienced both the positive and negative effects of the power of clothes. Each child has had a special relationship with clothes. For Ben, clothing created struggles that usually were terminated only by great emotional displays. The sock, yet a small article of clothing, posed one of the biggest hindrances to Ben's successful wearing of clothes. You see, if the seam over the toes of his sock did not line up perfectly with the part between the toe and the foot thus creating an appropriate feel, the sock would be ripped off only to be put on again. This continued over and over until a proper fit was achieved.

Matt provided us with a more laid-back approach to the wearing of clothes. He cared more about putting on clothes in order to create a new persona. Thus, he donned the cape, mask, and big bedroom shoes, and flew through the house where he turned Batman into Mattman. The power of the cape was strong. When his discipleship-training teacher asked the class who the first man God made was, my three-year-old raised his hand confidently and replied, "Batman." Ben, quite disturbed by Matt's stories about Batman, would tell him, "That's not true." Before he laid down his cape, Matt had one more encounter. He told of the time that he and Batman went to see Jesus at His house, and then Matt came back home to be my boy. I guess that was how I got Matt.

Different occasions, of course, demanded different clothing, and that sometimes came at a great expense. There were play clothes, sports clothes or uniforms, school clothes, and church clothes, which definitely could not be worn to school. There were first-day-of-school clothes that were different from school clothes because they had to be newly purchased, and there were vacation clothes (I came up with that one). With two little boys so close in age who looked very much alike and who sometimes found it difficult to stay with their parents, I decided we would need vacation clothes. It didn't have to be a formal vacation. Just any time we went somewhere together where there would be great crowds of people together and great temptation for one of them, Matt, to meander away from us, they would be required to wear vacation clothes. This meant that the boys would wear the exact same shirt and pants as the other. The shirt would always be a solid bright color. If I lost one child, I could immediately look at the other child and would know what to look for in the crowd. As the boys grew, you can imagine that they rebelled against the vacation clothes. So when we took a cruise together, after Matt's high school graduation, I was quite surprised on our first excursion off the boat. Touring the Mayan ruins, the boys were walking ahead of me; and to my amazement, they both had on matching black T-shirts with khaki shorts. I called out to them, and before they could react, I shot a picture. Proof! The vacation clothes live on. They are still debating the issue with me since in the photo, Matt did have a long sleeve shirt in his hand that he had taken off because it had become hotter throughout the day.

The power of clothing in our family could also be understood within the context and evolution of acceptable clothing choices. I will just state upfront what the boys are well aware of: baggy pants were not acceptable. They were also quite willing to tell Dad that short swim trunks were not only unacceptable but were appalling. Getting to something less controversial, when the boys were young, it was quite acceptable when they dressed themselves to maybe have their shirt inside out or a striped shirt with plaid pants or a red shirt on with green pants—okay, maybe not that. But as the boys noticed the power of the clothes, these practices that were once acceptable became a thing of the past. Then color became very important. Ben would only wear white cleats, whereas Matt would only wear black cleats. Ben's shirt choices, even to this day, are white and black. Matt got stuck on the color wheel for several years and would only wear orange. His favorite college team was Clemson, so during sixth and seventh grade years, he wore an orange shirt almost every day. Thankfully, by eighth grade, Matt caught up to the power of the clothes and decided orange every day may not be cool. Thank heavens for peer pressure! Khaki jeans found a place in the evolution cycle, from not cool to cool. I struggled many days with Ben, in the first grade, about what he would wear. It seemed that only blue jeans were acceptable. But after receiving Jesus in his heart, Ben was a new creation, and he vehemently declared, "Jesus is in my heart, and if he thinks khaki jeans are okay, then so do I!" I really don't know what Jesus thinks of khaki jeans; but that day, I was blessed that Ben knew, and that was all he needed.

So how did clothes get so much power? We were not born with them, yet they have become a most necessary covering. That's it! Back to the beginning, Adam and Eve were both naked and knew no shame (Gen. 2:25). When they sinned, their eyes were opened. They became aware of their nakedness, and it caused shame. They made an attempt at the first clothing line, one with fig leaves, but it was not a sufficient covering. Therefore, God made garments of skin for Adam and Eve, and clothed them (Gen. 3:21). God clothed them. Adam and Eve tried to clothe themselves, but they were not able to fully cover the shame of the sin. To cover sin, to clothe completely, there had to be shedding of blood which formed the animal skins (Heb. 9:22).

The Bible is full of descriptions of the importance of clothing, from the priest's robes to the sackcloth of the mourner. The colors of blue, purple, and scarlet clothing, as well as the material choices of linen or wool, many times connote the status of the wearer. Not only does the Bible discuss physical clothing, but it also discusses clothing ourselves in a greater reality. Just as Adam and Eve were attempting only to cover their bodies with physical clothing, and missed the mark, we fail to see the whole purpose and power of the clothing that God desires for us to understand. The deeper reality of clothing is that God sent His Son to shed His blood to clothe us in righteousness—for a right relationship with God. Isaiah 61:10 says, "I delight greatly in the Lord, my soul rejoices in my God, for he has clothed me with garments of salvation and arrayed me in a robe of righteousness."

Before becoming a chaplain in the Air Force, my husband was a civilian pastor. Then, his uniform, or clothing choice, was a coat and tie. On his first day as an active duty chaplain, Greg was carefully and eagerly putting on his crisp camouflage uniform and boots when our two-year-old strolled into the room, looked at his dad, and questioned, "Where are you going?" Proudly, Greg announced that he was going to work. Our son grinned, shook his head as if not to be outsmarted, and countered with, "No, you aren't going to work. You're going to shoot the birds." To Ben, if you look like you are going hunting, you are going hunting. It seems simple, but God warned us in Matthew 7:15 that people would wear false clothing, looking like one thing on the outside yet being wolves in reality. We must be one or the other. We must choose.

Every day, we put on clothes. We choose which clothes to put on. We also teach our children to put on clothes even though when they are young, they sometimes take them off at inconvenient times. In the same way that we choose physical clothes that sometimes look nice and sometimes look hideous, we also have a choice in our spiritual clothing. We can choose to clothe ourselves in shame and disgrace (Ps. 35:26, 109:29) or in strength and dignity (Prov. 31:25). We can choose to clothe ourselves with gloom and terror (Ezek. 31:15, 26:16) or with righteousness and justice (Job 29:14). We can choose to clothe ourselves with despair and violence (Ezek. 7:27, Ps. 73:6) or with compassion, kindness, gentleness, patience, and humility (Col. 3:12, 1 Pet. 5:5)

How then do we choose? How do we know we are wearing the right clothing? Remember how Adam and Eve tried to clothe themselves with the fig leaves but it didn't hide the shame of their sin? Second Corinthians 5:2–3 explains, "Meanwhile we groan, longing to be clothed with our heavenly dwelling, because when we are clothed we will not be found naked." We all have a deep longing for something to fill us properly, so we try clothes or many other things to make us feel accepted or to give us the power in our lives that we need. But nothing that perishes works; we just try a different set of imperishable clothes. But the Bible tells us that "the perishable must clothe itself with the imperishable" (1 Cor. 15:53). The answer to our need is to "clothe yourselves in the Lord Jesus Christ" (Rom. 13:14). Jesus shed His blood on the cross to cover our sin; God found that sacrifice acceptable as covering for our sin.

One of the gifts Matt received for his second birthday was a batting helmet used for baseball. There were no toddler helmets found in the stores, so we just got him the smallest size we could. Although the helmet swallowed his head so he couldn't even see and wobbled ferociously as he batted, Matt was thrilled that he had a baseball helmet. With the helmet, Matt was prepared for the ballgame even before he would be old enough to play. When he was four years old, he could not understand why Ben got to play soccer and he did not. The rules of the league prohibited four-year-olds from playing. We lived in Turkey at the time, so there were no other leagues with which to be involved. Matt begged to have a soccer uniform, so we complied and found one at the Base Exchange. Every time Ben had a game, Matt would go to the game dressed in his uniform and stand on the sidelines, kicking the ball around—ready to be put in. After all, he was dressed. I reminded him often that he was not old enough to play, but he would say, "Mom, if Coach sees me in uniform and knows I am ready, one day, he may need me. He may put me in." I believed him. Matt was ready to play, and he was prepared with the right clothing to be put in the game. Matt's desire to be ready makes me wonder: why not put on the right clothes now? Why not be prepared to play? Why are we waiting for another time?

I am sure that you have pictures of your children when they were babies or toddlers in various degrees of dress that when they become teenagers and saw what you did, they are appalled. Flipping through picture books recently, Matt saw a picture of himself playing in the neighbor's yard clothed with just diapers and a shirt. Needless to say, he was not impressed that I had not properly outfitted him. All I heard was, "How could you do that? How could you let me run around in public undressed?" Telling him he was two didn't soften the blow to his ego. Allowing Matt to wear diapers outside was one thing I could live with. But if later in life my children were to come to me and ask why I didn't show them how to be clothed in Christ, that would be a travesty.

As parents, we are responsible to clothe our children. We teach them what to wear and what not to wear, but we miss the mark if we only talk about the covering of our physical bodies. We need to teach them to put on Christ so they can be prepared and play in this race of life, not just sitting on the sidelines. Wearing costumes at the Harvest Festivals at the chapel were always so much fun for the boys. Because our boys loved Bibleman, a fictional Bible superhero, our costumes usually consisted of swords, shields, and lots of trouble. I love how the Bible lays out clearly and visually for us as parents how to dress and how to teach our children to dress. "Put on the full armor of God, so that when the day of evil comes you may be able to stand your ground, and after you have done everything to stand. Stand firm then, with the belt of truth buckled around your waist, with the breastplate of righteousness in place and with your feet fitted with the readiness that comes from the gospel of peace. In addition to all this, take up the shield of faith, with which you can extinguish all the flaming arrows of the evil one. Take the helmet of salvation and the sword of the Spirit which is the word of God" (Eph. 6:13–17).

The summer between Matt's junior and senior years of high school, he flew to Arizona from New Mexico to play in a baseball showcase. He was so excited because he was flying alone. He wanted to get to the airport much earlier than his flight so he could wander around the terminal and mostly go to Starbucks and get coffee by himself. After the trip, Matt enthusiastically and quite proudly reported to me that people in the airport both times thought he was in the military. When I asked him why they might have thought this, he pointed to his clothes. He was wearing an Air Force T-shirt, a camo backpack, and of course, his haircut was short. Then I asked how he knew they thought that. He humbly disclosed the conversation. "They thanked me for my service, and I said, 'You are welcome.'" Matt is a military kid who did serve all his life moving every two to three years following his dad all over the world. He dressed the part. He looked the part, and he was ready to serve.

What kind of power is in the clothes you wear, and what are you clothing your children with? It may be time to clean out the closet, throw out the old, and bring on the new and more powerful clothes.

Backpack Time

That same sick feeling was back. It started in the pit of my stomach and then moved up to my throat, almost choking me. It hurt, so of course, I started crying. It was grief, and it attacked me every year about the same time. No, it was not the anniversary of the loss of a loved one or a tragic event in my life. It was not a memory of anything. It was the beginning of something. I knew it should not induce these feelings, but it did. The rest of the world, the stores, and many other parents would look forward to this time with anticipation; but I didn't. I dreaded it every single year because it marked the end of fun. It marked the end of summer. It was back-to-school time!

All summer long, the boys and I spent time together endlessly relaxing, playing, and enjoying all their summer sports and exploring new adventures. Then it would abruptly come to a halt! Someone else—the school—demanded time with my children, and I didn't want to give them up. The last week before school, I selfishly tried to squeak out all the fun and excitement I could with the boys. In order to protect my emotional fragility during these days (and because it had become a ritual in our family), the boys would politely decline a friend's invitation during this week so they could play with Mama. The main event during this week was a day at the zoo, followed by bowling, the movies, going out to eat, and school shopping. But mainly, we just had a good time, laughed, cut up, and were together.

It was good to enjoy the fellowship of my boys. I knew I would let them go to school. Heaven forbid I considered homeschooling. It was just not my gift. I wanted them to go to school, and they equally wanted to go to school. But I had threatened homeschooling as punishment before. I guess this emptiness in the pit of my stomach and these tears running down my face just meant that I love my boys, and I love spending time with them. It is good that I should miss my boys. As it did every year, the pain would lessen, the routine would begin, and I would cherish and look forward to everyday afterschool when I could share in the events, excitement, and drama of each school day. And of course, Labor Day was a holiday, and then came fall break, and Christmas was right around the corner.

My boys never attended preschool, so I vividly remember the first day I took Ben to kindergarten. It was eight in the morning when Matt and I walked Ben to the small classroom at the church school where seven other kindergarten students sat ready to start their life of learning. Ben walked boldly into the classroom acting as if he had done this all his life. Matt and I strolled back to the car without Ben, and then I let loose. I wailed out loud, heaving and shaking as if I had just left my son forever. Dumbfounded by my behavior, Matt, who was almost two years behind Ben, questioned, "Mom, we are coming back to get him, aren't we?" "Well, of course we are! We will be back by the stroke of noon or most likely before." But that was not the problem. I knew this was just the beginning of many times I would leave without Ben. Even if just for four hours, I would miss him.

The house was very quiet now. The clocks and washing machine were making noises. I didn't even realize how much noise they made days ago when boys' loud voices covered every other noise. Today was the first day of school—again. I know what you are thinking: "This lady is wacko! She needs to get a life outside of the time she spends with her children." Don't worry; I have one. I love and adore the time I spend with my husband first. I have lots of friends, and I volunteer endlessly with church and women's groups. I am a social worker by trade, but currently a stay-at-home mom by choice. I know that many are not able to make this choice, so I am forever grateful that I was able to choose. So from the chaperoning of school field trips (for which the boys owe me big, especially the Boonie Stomp through the jungles of Guam) to the joys of snow days with the compulsory hot chocolate, marshmallows, and movies, I am grateful. I am willing to sacrifice a little "me" time for a lot of "us" time. This time together builds a connection—a relationship.

"Loving time" was what we first called it. Every night, we climbed on a bed together as a family, we called it a boat, read a Bible story or a Bible-story book, and laughed and talked together. This was a great time of telling and listening. The boys soon realized I was a sucker for sharing, so I let them believe they were achieving their end—the more sharing they did, the longer they got to stay up. In reality I was achieving my end—fellowship with the family and the opportunity to learn the thoughts and hearts of these two little people. Then we prayed.

Time together was important so throughout their changing lives, we capitalized on finding this precious fellowship. When Ben was six years old, every day, I met him at the bus stop. Our walk home set a precedent for afterschool sharing that continued in some form until they each graduated from high school. Throughout the elementary years, we had backpack time. Each day after school, I sat in Greg's chair; and each boy, one after the other, revealed the contents of his backpack all while telling of the day's events. It was during this backpack time the boys learned to express frustrations, opinions, and thoughts that were so very important in the life of a little boy; and a mom listened, pondered, laughed, and enjoyed a growing relationship during backpack time.

Middle school and high school brought more sophisticated talks and more varied places in which to fellowship. Many times, I picked Matt up from school; and we would sit in the car in the garage for minutes to hours, reviewing each class, dissecting each story of personal hurt or achievement, and rehearsing each joy and dream. The love couch, as Ben and Matt called it, was a small love seat in the front room of the house in Colorado Springs. On that small inexpensive piece of furniture, life's problems were solved, feelings were shared, and I got the scoop on what was happening in the lives of my teenage boys. On that couch, we had fellowship, grew in rela-tionship, and learned to trust and cherish each other.

Twice now, our family of four, three of who are men ranging in size from six feet two inches to six feet six inches, had piled in a pickup truck, looking much like the Beverly Hillbillies, to drive from New Mexico to South Carolina to deliver students to college. Even though I was relegated to the back seat behind the driver the entire trip while the others shared rotating seating, I looked forward to this compact time of fellowship! So before our last trip together in the truck when my youngest son, who was also the largest, volunteered, no begged, to fly and meet us in South Carolina, I insisted we pack in and enjoy the ride—together. I knew that our times together as a family would be fewer and fewer, so I took advantage of whatever time I had together, even if it was pretty uncomfortable!

Since the boys left for college, we had less time to spend together physically; so when Ben was home one break and asked me to sit down and watch a television program with him, I stopped everything. I watched *Bully Beat Down, Top Shot*, and whatever else Ben wanted to share with me. I don't know if he really thought I would enjoy the programs, but he wanted to fellowship with me, and I with him. Once when Matt was home from college, I noticed he was holding one of his children's Bible storybooks. He grabbed my hand and asked me to sit on the couch next to him as he read me his favorite story from our "loving time" days. Both times, while on the couch fellowshipping with my young-adult sons in the way they chose, I realized they were paying me back with time. They wanted relationship. They wanted fellowship. They had learned to practice that perfect blessing of time given to one another.

I enjoy the fellowship with my children! I like being with them. No matter how hard it is to parent some days. No matter how messy and disobedient the boys are at times, I like being with them. This should be a goal of parenting to enjoy our children and the time we spend with them. God created us for fellowship. He created us in His image to have fellowship with Him. In the Old Testament, God so wanted to enjoy the fellowship of His creation that He instructed them to make the tabernacle so His presence could dwell with His people. The completed plan of God was in Christ where with Him, our joy and fellowship could be complete. First John 1:3 says, "We proclaim to you what we have seen and heard, so that you also may have fellowship with us and our fellowship is with the Father and with his Son, Jesus, Christ." John Piper, in his book *Desiring God*, wrote, "The chief aim of man is to glorify God by enjoying Him forever."

It is hard to fathom that God has allowed us to participate in His creative process by making children that are in our likeness. When Matt was only four, he came to me with a stark revelation: "Mama, I just found out that I have to like you 'cause you're the only mom I am getting. And Ben said it's true." Even through the mixed feelings about the comment, I had to be grateful that, "Yep, you got me, kid, and I have you!" The fellowship and relationship with each other is in the image of the glorious and faithful relationship and fellowship we have with our Father God.

When Matt was very young, his request for fellowship was simple. He would always ask for "half an a minute." One night, when kissing Ben good night, he posed a question. "Do you have a half an hour you could spare?" Every "half an a minute" or even half an hour they asked for, I tried to give. Every minute is worth the fellowship so the relationship will grow! Put down the book for "half an a minute" and go enjoy your children forever.

"We Gotta Pray"

It was a bittersweet visit at the end of January 1998. The sweet was an early celebration of my birthday with my parents; the bitter came as they helped us process the new assignment the Air Force had just given Greg. As our first assignment at Moody Air Force base in Valdosta, Georgia, was coming to an end, Greg had just been informed that he had been selected for a remote assignment to Korea for a year, without his family. He would be expected to report the first part of April. For the three years that Greg had been on active duty, combining all the time he had been gone with deployments, special assignments, and classes, he had already been away from us for about a year. The prospect of him going to Korea was overwhelming especially with three- and five-year-old boys. Before Mama and Daddy came to visit Greg, and I had worked through our shock and had given the assignment back to the Lord, realizing that He had given it to us. Knowing God and His love for us, we understood that He must have a plan for us in this assignment. On this particular day, Greg was to call the assignments personnel to inform them of his desired follow on assignment. Mama and Daddy, Ben and Matt, and I were sitting at the lunch table before their trip back home when Greg called. My silent listening erupted into screams, laughter, and tears as I heard from Greg that someone had volunteered to go to Korea in his place and that they were sending us to Turkey—TOGETHER—AS A FAMILY. Through the uproar of three adults screeching and crying and talking, my three-year-old son, Matt, offered up the most profound admonition in a voice that quieted this boisterous group. "We gotta pray," was all he said, so we did. We bowed our heads and led by a three-year-old, thanked our God who does more than we can ever ask, think, or imagine.

That day around the lunch table, Matt didn't understand what was going on. With all the different emotions being displayed at once, he didn't even know if a good thing was happening or a bad thing was happening, but it didn't matter. He knew what to do in any situation, and he knew it early in his life. As soon as the boys were learning to talk and to listen, they were learning to pray. Just as they grew in depth and understanding in their communication with us as parents, they grew in depth and understanding of prayer. As with all learning, prayer took practice, so we did.

I chronicled many prayers in my boys' journey. From the time they were babies, we would fold their little hands and ask a blessing for our food, so after the first time, we began nighttime prayers with Matt folding his hands; it was no surprise that he concluded our prayer with, "Amen. Eat?" He then grew to his prayer at twenty-three months. "Thank you, Jesus, for ba—ball" (translation: baseball). It didn't take long for the boys to figure out that prayers were not only for thanking God, but also for asking for stuff. You can imagine with that newfound understanding, their prayer life took off!

Ben made quick use of this new found awareness, and at three years old, was asking, "Jesus, help me learn my numbers so I can get a calculator." (Jesus probably knew that was the prerequisite for getting a calculator.) While Ben began to mix thanksgiving with his requests: "Dear Heavenly Father, thank you for the Bible. I love your stories. Lord, can I be a scientist?" Matt continued with requests mixed with a bit of tattle telling on parents: "Jesus, I can't have a dog 'cause I haven't learned not to pull their tail." Or, "Dear Jesus, I am sad 'cause Mama won't give me anything to eat. Could you help her?"

Matt was learning two important aspects of prayer: tell God your feelings and prayer does work. He had lost his original construction paper starfish, which was his ticket to ride the kindergarten bus, so I made him a new one. I made him a pink starfish because I thought I had remembered that his original one was pink and made it the same just in case the color was of importance to the teacher. I pinned it on Matt before school, and he never said a word. Before we walked to the bus stop, we all stopped to pray for our day, and Matt led, "Dear Lord, please don't let any of my friends laugh at me because I am wearing a pink starfish." The Lord heard and answered. I took the starfish off his shirt and put it in his pocket, just in case he needed it.

They were still just little boys growing. Learning to communicate, learning to listen. But they were maturing in their knowledge of God as they talked to him and learned of him. Their world expanded and so did their prayers. When we lived in Turkey, the Muslim Imam chanted prayers over the loud speaker five times a day for all to hear. One night, my four-year-old Matt in his prayers asked, "Jesus, help me tell that man about you."

When Ben was four, he also began thinking of prayer as a way to help outside of himself. We had concluded our prayer time and "loving time" as we called it. One night, when Ben felt compelled to add, he said, "I got one more thing to tell, God. Dear Lord, some kids don't have houses and food to eat. Please, please, please get people to build them houses and get them a store, not with candy, but with lots of healthy food."

Not only were my little boys learning to consider others in their prayers, but they were pondering just who is God. "One day, I will get to see you," prayed my four-year-old. "I hope you love everybody today. I hope you see everybody at one time." Another night he prayed, "I believe God, but I can't see you. I hope you have a good day. Love me and Mama and Daddy and Ben and everybody in the universe. And please come pick us up before I die."

The questions about prayer came regularly as we practiced this sacrament in our home. "I know God doesn't listen to bad kids' prayers, but if a kid is nice and good but didn't ask forgiveness, does God listen?" Since that question was posed by my five-year-old, I was apprehensive about the questions that would flood as they grew even more, so we kept talking to God every day and every night and about everything.

At six years old, Ben began to learn something about prayer that would continue through his life. "Thank you for my self-control." Pausing to giggle, he added, "I really like having self-control because I don't get into punishment so much now." At ten, Ben divulged this truth about prayer. "Mom, when I pray all the time, I feel real

good. But when I stop praying, I feel the world is getting in me."
Ben began to see a pattern related to prayer: I noticed Ben began to
leave his bedroom shoes by his bed every night. His explanation, "I
put them there to remind me to pray each morning that God will
help me make good choices. This prayer thing really is helping. I
am going to pray seven or nine times a day." The boys were learning
that prayer works. Ben was almost six when we first read the Bible
story of Esther during our family devotions. After Greg and I left
the boys' room and turned off the light, Ben timidly walked into the
den and reported that Matt really wanted to see us. As I was going
to comfort Matt, Ben passed by me on the way to the bedroom and
said, "Mom, guess what I did? I asked God not to let you spank me
before I went in to see you. And he did! That's just like Esther when
she prayed before she went to see the king." At eleven years old, Ben
came home from school and immediately grabbed my hand, took
me back to his bedroom and softly said, "Mom, I've got to tell you
something." As I braced myself for Ben's comments, he showed me a
progress report that he assumed would not bring a favorable reaction.
Instead, I calmly questioned him and said we would work through
it, and everything would be okay. Suddenly, a smile burst on his face
as he exclaimed, "IT WORKKS!" Then he continued, "Mom, I have
been praying for you all day that God would help me tell you this
and that you would be okay with it. It really worked!" What a lesson!
Prayer works! "If God can help Mom receive a bad grade this calmly,
then He can do anything!" In my heart, I was compelled to pray,
"Thank you, Lord, for restraining me so that you could teach Ben
that prayer works."

When Matt was a toddler, and beyond, at least a thousand
times a day with his signature slow drawl, he asked, "Ma...ma, can
I taaawlk to you?" And at least a thousand times a day, I stopped
and said, "Of course!" My children understood from the very beginning that I would listen to them as they talked. Nothing was off
limits, and I encouraged them that they could also ASK anything.
Ironically, many times, they put limits on my listening as they were
asking their questions of me. I was often chided that I could not say
anything until they were completely finished with their request. At

times, I was not even allowed to look at them as they approached me with their appeal. Prior to their entreaties, many times, the boys had a ritual of begging; "Please, please, please," just to grease the slide for their upcoming inquiry. I always wondered why they felt such trepidation before asking me—their parent who loved them and always encouraged them to ask me anything—for something they desired. The boys learned as they kept asking that I would respond to their requests in love. Through our practice of communicating and building a trusting relationship where the boys knew me and trusted my faithfulness to them, we were modeling the practice of prayer. Psalm 142:2 says, "I pour out my complaint before him, before him I tell my trouble." First John 5:14–15 states, "This is the confidence we have in approaching God: that if we ask anything according to his will: he hears us. And if we know that he hears us—whatever we ask—we know that we have what we asked of him." As the boys grew older, they've matured in their ability to ask for desires, share their hurts, and communicate their joys. As our communication matures with our children, so will their understanding of their confidence to communicate with their heavenly Father.

The disciples were around Jesus constantly. They learned to trust Him, to communicate with Him. But even with that constant relationship, they asked him, "Teach us to pray" (Luke 11:1). We may model a relationship where children learn to trust their parents so they can ask their parents anything, but we still need to TEACH them to pray. Teach them that God wants to hear what they say, teach them that God wants to hear how they feel, teach them that God will answer them, and teach them that God listens to them. Teach them just as Jesus taught the disciples to pray. "Our Father in heaven, reveal who you are, set the world right, Do what's best—as above, so below. Keep us alive with three square meals. Keep us forgiven with you and forgiving others. Keep us safe from ourselves and the Devil. You're in charge! You can do anything you want! You're ablaze in beauty!" (Matt. 6:9–13, *The Message*). When we teach them to pray, we will be teaching them to know God, to talk to God, to rely on God, and to listen to God. And as we teach them, they will also teach us. One day, I was scolded by my very young Ben, "Mom,

Jesus talks to me. And if you will be quiet and listen, He will talk to you." Then I began to listen more fervently to their prayers in order that I might learn, from the mouths of children, the heart of God. Matt's prayer at five years old illustrated the substance of all our prayers: "Thank you, Jesus, for saving my mama, daddy, and Ben."

As the boys' prayers evolved, so did mine. I must confess that many times, I have had some seemingly earthly prayers: "Please let Matt throw strikes or at least change the umpire's strike zone to coincide with where Matt is throwing the ball. Please let the boys grow tall and big. Please let the boys make the honor roll even without counting gym class. Please let the boys behave in church since their dad is the preacher and their mom is playing the keyboard." I did mix these prayers with more mature prayers: "Above all, help them to know Jesus, to love Him, and to love His word. Help them make good choices. Guide them in choosing a life partner that loves and follows you." But many times, as they were growing, problems would come, and I wouldn't know what to pray. When Matt was young one night during prayers, he only said a two-word prayer, so he explained, "My tongue is tired and sore. That's why I can't say my prayers" Often, it seemed that my tongue was tired, and I didn't know how to pray. But God even had an answer to my lack of words: "In the same way the Spirit helps us in our weakness. We do not know what we ought to pray for, but the Spirit himself intercedes for us with groans that words cannot express" (Rom. 8:26). God taught me to pray for my children by using His words, so as I would read through the scripture, I would put a triangle by every verse that could be used as a verse for my children. I prayed for Ben and Matt alone, I prayed for Ben and Matt with my husband Greg, and I prayed for Ben and Matt with other mothers at Moms in Touch and other women's groups. I took literally the verse, "Pray without ceasing" (1 Thess. 5:17). I realized early in the boys' lives that I was overwhelmed with the responsibility of being a mom. I could not do everything for them, I could not be everywhere with them, I could not make good choices for them. But when I could not, I could surrender them to prayer to someone who could and who would. So I prayed!

I often used a book written by Stormie Omartian called, *The Power of a Praying Parent*. After years of use, the book is totally marked up, cried on, and tattered; but recently, I gave it to my twenty-one-year-old son Matt and told him, "These are the things I have prayed for you all your life. Now you pray them for you." Don't worry. I didn't stop praying for the boys. I just graduated as I found her book, *The Power of Praying for Your Adult Children*. Prayer for my children never ends—and I will have daughters-in-law and grandchildren to add. It seems that young children increased my physical muscles, but grown children have definitely increased my praying muscles. I was encouraged by Samuel who proclaimed to his people, the children of Israel, "As for me, far be it from me that I should sin against the Lord by failing to pray for you. And I will teach you the way that is good and right" (1 Sam. 12:23). I saw it as my duty to hold up Ben and Matt throughout their life, and the only way I could do that successfully was and is through prayer. In Exodus 12, there is an account of Joshua in a battle. As long as Moses's hands were up in the air, Joshua was winning; but as Moses's hands grew tired and they dropped, Joshua began to lose the battle. Moses then sat on a stone, and two men came alongside Moses, one on each side, to lift his arms and keep them up during the battle. Joshua defeats the enemy. As a mom, I am lifting up the arms of Ben and Matt through battle so they can win the war.

I didn't always parent correctly, but I prayed. Sometimes I forgot, and sometimes I prayed the wrong thing, and sometimes my mouth was tired and my heart didn't know what to say. But the reward of seeing my high school son kneeling by his bed praying and the privilege of receiving a call from my college son asking for prayer became the highest reward because these boys for whom I have prayed, pray!

Performance and Competition

My baby was only six months old, and the lady at church who had a baby six months earlier was quizzing me. "When did he roll over? Is he smiling yet? But my baby is already crawling. My baby is already eating cereal. My baby is already blah blah blah." I ended up not liking her or her baby. What were these new feelings exploding within me? I started judging my baby according to what he could do, so the stress began. The pressure began. The world had infiltrated my thoughts. The sneaky presumption that children must perform and do something more, something bigger, or something better in order to be special has snuck its way into the psyche of moms everywhere and has begun an ugly work.

Sadly, it gets worse because it does not end. Like a metastasizing cancer, this pattern of thought flourishes with each new age and with each new interest or activity. "My child won the science fair. Well, my child made all A's this quarter. Oh, your son is not in AP classes? You mean he is taking college math and not Calculus?" And as a sports mom, I had to bite my tongue more than once. "What is your son's 60 time? How fast is his fastball? How many Division 1 offers does he have? Oh, he is going to a junior college?" This performance worldview has no prejudices and no limits, and it must be exposed!

The day my child was born, the competition began. Many people asked me how much he weighed. How long was he? Immediately, the thought was placed in my head that there must be a "right" or "good" answer to that question, but I only had a truthful answer. And because my babies were large at birth, I felt that gave me extra credit in the mom department. When they were born, the nurses would say they would probably not grow as fast since they were born big. That didn't happen, so immediately, for some reason, I felt a sense of pride and competition with the nurse who somehow I had proved wrong by the boys growing. Of course, right on schedule, I went to the pediatrician with Ben, and the first thing they did encouraged positive performance. They brought out a height-and-weight chart and measured Ben against the standard. I always got to walk out of the doctor's office with great pride as my boys exceeded the expectation of the chart! In some twisted way, I was rewarded by the performance of my boys, and all they had done was eat and grow. With my sick sort of pride, I was always eager for the next yearly check up to see how far my boys had come, as if I couldn't see.

I was not the only one to ask the question: could the standard ever be wrong? Matt, at his five-year-old pediatrician visit before attending kindergarten, was asked to step next to the indicator displayed on the wall that was used to document growth in height. The measurements were recorded in his chart, but upon looking at the results taken by the technician, the undersized doctor requested that Matt be measured again. Still not agreeing with the results, the doctor, who suggested this could not be accurate, did something I had never seen before. He measured himself at the indicator displayed on the wall and seemed puzzled when his height was assessed correctly. My neighbor was one of the doctors in this pediatrician's office and later commented to me an odd need that was brought up in the staff meeting. This pediatrician proposed the staff find a new way to measure the height of children. It seemed that the yardstick did not work anymore. Just because this pediatrician could not accept that Matt greatly exceeded the standard height set for a five-year-old boy, he thought maybe the way of measuring was wrong.

Many years later, we found ourselves at yet another doctor visit. This time, it was a high school sport's physical. Ben, a junior, was first. He came in at a healthy 6'1" and 155 pounds. The observant medical technician aptly declared that since Ben was in the ninety-five percentile in height and seventy-five percentile in weight, according to the standard, that he was tall and lean. Matt, a freshman, was next. He scored a 6'3" with 200 pounds, which once again blew the standard and put him above the one-hundred percentile in each category. We waited expectantly for the technician's brilliant deductive assessment of Matt's numbers, but nothing came. We waited in silence. Matt finally broke the penetrating quiet and asked, "Well, what does that make me?" The unwelcome answer was returned by a question, "Proportional?" My boys can't be defined by a standard imposed by someone else—not even a growth chart.

Having to live in the world, but not be of the world, we embraced the competition but tried hard not to define our boys by the prevailing expectations imposed. Thus, we jumped in with all gusto and encouraged the boys to try as many activities as possible. Baseball was their first endeavor. At the ripe ages of one and three, the boys began to learn America's game. They packed up bats and gloves in an "official" baseball bag: balls in the tennis-ball carrier, a batting helmet that engulfed their whole head, and of course, the Big League Chew (gum); and headed out to the baseball field near our house for a boy's day out adventure. Swinging the bat and actually hitting the ball earned each boy the opportunity to run the bases, being chased by Daddy, and squealing all the way. The boys were hooked! By the time they were three years old, they were playing on an organized baseball team. From YMCA leagues to Air Force Base leagues, to Little League, to Competitive travel leagues, to high school baseball, and then college baseball, baseball became our favorite pastime.

Soccer was a short-lived activity. Ben played a couple of years, but Matt quickly assessed his chances for effective competition and determined, "Mom, my feet are too big for this game." I knew there were other complications for his competent play, but being the gracious mom, I concurred with his appraisal and challenged him elsewhere—basketball! Matt and Ben played in Upward Basketball Leagues for years, and then after middle school, Ben stopped to con-centrate on baseball; but Matt continued with many travel leagues and through high school.

The last of the big-three sports was football—so why not add that? After all, I'm sure I would not want a single season of the year not dedicated to a sport! For football, we at least waited until our move to Guam when the boys were in the fourth and sixth grades. They arrived at the field the first day of practice only to be surrounded by a group of wide-eyed Chamorro boys looking up at Ben and Matt questioning, "Are all the boys on the mainland big like you?" But as soon as their local coach heard the inquiry, he quickly justified the difference in the standard by saying, "We are shorter on the island because of the sun." What?

It may sound like the boys only tried their competitive hand at sports, but they did try other things—Ben the trumpet, piano, guitar, and gymnastics. And Matt, well, he likes to sing. But it didn't take long for them to discern that they **loved** to play sports, and they **liked** other things. So we plunged head first into the competitive waters and forged ahead with baseball, basketball, and football. From these, we have gleaned many lessons about competition, performance, expectations, ourselves, and the great gifts of God.

The sun was hot at high noon as Ben stood on the mound pitching in a game that had the Anderson Air Force A's up after the first three innings in the battle against the best local team in Guam's Little League. It was as if the whole island had come to cheer on the home team in the contest against the military kids. The game turned ugly in the fourth inning when the home plate umpire chose to participate in the outcome. Ben continued to pitch, as I being the ever-faithful mom, continued to record every pitch. As the ball came over the plate, the player did not swing and the umpire called, "Ball." Over and over, the boys for the other team did not swing, the umpire called, "Ball." The Guam team walked to first base, then to second, then to third. Even though Ben was throwing many strikes, the coaches tried a new pitcher to test the umpire, only to encounter the same result. After forty-five minutes and five pitchers later, the umpire decided to resume proper calling, but only after the score had risen to an insurmountable count. Greg, who was coaching at the time, tried to talk to the umpire but was directed that if he said a word, he would be thrown out of the game. Our fifth-, sixth-, and seventh-grade Little Leaguers lost the game in a big way that day. In the world's view, they were the losers; but as Greg said in his coach's after-game wrap up to the boys, "I am so proud of you today. You experienced a prejudice in your life today and stood up strong in the midst of it. Remember this experience today. Don't be angry. You won!"

As a big boy all of his life, Matt had to overcome high expectations when it came to sports performance. Many people assumed he was older and so expected older behavior. Others thought that he just naturally was able to play up with the older boys. What they didn't see were the hours and hours in a gym in order to play varsity basketball at a 5A school just because the coach said in order to play, one had to be able to make fifty three-point shots in five minutes. The standard or expectation had been set, so Matt, even though a big man, shot threes until he mastered his craft and made the varsity team as a sophomore. Practice, sacrifice, extra work was what it took to perform to the standard set, and he was rewarded this time. But several years later, at another high school, a new coach came in with no stated standard for playing. Matt would start the game or not start the game randomly and would be pulled or put in not knowing where he stood in regard to his performance. Totally frustrated after a big game where there was no clear standard for playing time, Matt picked up a basketball as people were leaving the gym and began to shoot. The only thing he said to me with hurt yet determined eyes was, "I will be my best for this team—whatever that looks like." One by one, the spectators of the game left, the cheerleaders left, the referees left, the principal left, the athletic director and the coaches came to the gym door one by one as if trying to sneak a peek without being noticed. As the janitor began to sweep the other end of the gym floor, the only ones left were Greg feeding Matt balls and me sitting on the bleachers, eyes watering with pride and heart breaking with hurt. A man who had noticed this taking place came over to me and said, "He will be alright." And he was! He practiced not for an arbitrary standard, because none was set. He practiced to make himself the best he could be—for himself and for the team.

Each August for football, November for basketball, and February for baseball, Ben and Matt had to grapple with being judged against a sea of competitors for a position on the team. For weeks before his first high school baseball tryouts, Ben had been taunted by a teammate he had to play behind in summer ball and summer all-stars. Although Ben knew if given an objective tryout, he could play ahead of this teammate, he slumped in the car after the first day of tryouts, exhausted and admitting, "I am afraid." All the competing scenarios piled up, thus creating for Ben an almost unbearable weight of fear. Yet he and Matt stood up under this over and over, only to discover that comments from other people could not determine who they were or what they could do. The fear, though real and overwhelming, did not defeat.

Matt pitched his first four-inning game at ten years old. He usually only threw two innings. After the game, which we won 12-6, the home plate umpire brought a ball to Matt and asked him to sign it. "'Cause one day you will be in the pros," he said. Matt looked at me, took the ball, said thanks, and signed it. That night in his prayers, he gave voice to this understanding. "Lord, you know after the first inning I pitched, I was worried about the shifting of my weight, my release point, what the coaches told me to do, and my stride. But I just realized it was you who gives me my strength to pitch, so I decided to think about you instead. Then I thank you that I started throwing strikes." I continue to give voice to the knowledge that competition and performance has not tainted my boys but has taught them the gift of relying on the God that created them.

As my boys competed and learned, I learned. I learned that our twentieth-year anniversary plans take second place to a trip to Arkansas with a vanload of eleven-year-old Little League all-stars headed to regional's. I learned that if you stuff dryer sheets in baseball uniforms, mosquitoes would not bite. I learned that doctor visits for black eyes, sprained ankles, concussions, and bruised ribs would be many. I learned that bathrooms at baseball and football fields and basketball courts were great places to pray. I learned that reviewing scripture on index cards during a game could ease anxiety; and I learned, to the dismay of my boys, that my Southern accent stood out in a crowd in New Mexico and Colorado.

As a fifth grader on the mound, Matt was struggling to throw strikes. The coach, determined to calm him down in this important game, approached the mound and told Matt to just relax, take it easy, stretch, be calm, and just throw. The coach walked back to the dugout, and Matt stretched his arm, threw the ball—it was a strike! Before the next pitch, Matt stretched his legs, threw the ball—it was a strike! Employing his newfound relaxation technique, I expected Matt, before his next pitch, to lie on the mound in a yoga pose in order to stretch his back. My child was a literalist. He would try to do exactly what you say. By seeing Matt and Ben compete—by seeing them perform compared to the supposed standard of the day—I learned who my boys were and who they are becoming.

Matt had played football for two years in Guam before our moving to Colorado. He had always wanted to play quarterback but was only put on the offensive line in Guam since he was so much larger than the other boys. Because as a lineman, Matt did not touch the ball, he failed to see how that was even playing a game. He was so excited when seventh grade football tryouts arrived. Leaving home that morning, he declared, "I am gonna play quarterback!" All the way to school, I tried to prepare Matt with the realities of the situation and encouraged him that if he made the team, he should just play the position the coach deemed best. Unhindered by my cautions, Matt repeated his dream, "I'm gonna be quarterback this time." Curious about the competition, I parked close to the field during the tryouts so I could see, but remained unseen. To my dismay, sixty boys were lined up to try out just for the quarterback position! I didn't even watch the practice, but instead rehearsed my speech for Matt when he informed me he was relegated to play the line again. So distracted by my thoughts, I jumped when Matt nonchalantly plopped in the car and announced that he was the quarterback. Competition, performance, and the need to reach a standard of excellence created in my boys' lives hopes, dreams, and ambitions that propelled them to reach far beyond even my expectations. I learned that day, when my confident little boy became quarterback for his middle school football team, that accomplishing his hopes and dreams would far outweigh any obstacles that would stand in his way. He, and I, would need that lesson for the road ahead.

Being forced to live in this performance-based world with my boys sometimes brought out feelings and behaviors that should stay hidden. I will confess that I have, on more than one occasion, stared down a coach with the evil eye—without him knowing it, of course. I have ruined many a manicure. I have avoided obnoxious braggadocios parents in the stands. I have strained my voice while yelling at referees. I have sometimes even been less than cordial with the boys' teammates who I felt were coming between Ben and Matt and their dreams. This confession is not making me feel better about whom I have been in the midst of the boys' competition. I believe it is worse because of my instinctual desire to protect, defend, and build up at all cost. But during one of Greg's less than stellar moments, a truth resonated loudly. We were at a high school basketball game in Albuquerque, New Mexico. The other team had been consistently pounding Matt with fouls all night with no referee intervention. Exasperated after Matt was called for an unfair foul violation, Greg, with great piety of cause, stood up and yelled loudly at the referee the only thing he could think to say, "Jesus sees what you are doing!" The crowd continued to yell, the referee continued to make bad calls. Though appalled at his dad's behavior, Matt continued to play. Although maybe an inappropriate way to share this truth of Jesus, I agreed that Jesus did see my behavior during the boys' competitions; and somehow, that made me smile and also repent.

The boys did not win every game. They did not start every game. Sometimes, they could not throw a strike over the plate. Sometimes, they struck out. Sometimes, they didn't get to play the position they wanted. Sometimes, no one threw them a pass. Sometimes, they could not make a free throw. Sometimes, they were disappointed. They were disappointed because somehow, they equated their performance with their worth. That's what the world does. That's what people tell them from the very beginning with every human standard they have been measured against. But God's judgments and His value of us are not performance based.

The Psalmist asks the question, "What is man that you are mindful of him, the son of man that you care for him? You have made him a little lower than the heavenly beings and crowned him with glory and honor. You have made him ruler over the works of your hands and put everything under his feet" (Ps. 8:4–6).

"How great is the love that the Father has lavished on us that we should be called the children of God. And that's what we are" (1 John 3:1)! That is what we are! The charts and standards of this world will never assign value to our children. God does. It's called love. Oswald Chambers said, "We cannot measure our life by success but only by what God pours through us, and we cannot measure that at all."

When our boys were toddlers, we asked them to say their ABCs over and over again. We asked them to sing the little songs they knew. We asked them to dance in front of total strangers. Through all their sweet, yet imperfect performances, we only noticed and applauded our adorable little boys, precious in our eyes, for which we lavished all our love. For the standard of love, there is no end; but as Ben admitted, there are rules while competing in this world I had better learn. As I was kissing his face one night when putting him to bed, he shared this thought, "Mom, you can kiss my face on and on until the earth explodes," he paused, "but don't kiss me at soccer."

Perspective—We All Need God's

When the boys were toddlers, between the fish tanks, the toy aisle, the snack bar, and the balls in the sporting goods section, Wal-Mart offered countless hours of entertainment. One afternoon, as the boys and I were walking to the car after our excursion, Ben noticed a long white streak in the sky. Obvious to me, it was a streak left by a plane; but to Ben, it was much more. When my four-year-old Ben saw the streak in the sky, he plainly and confidently explained from his perspective the significance of the white streak that now held our gaze. You see, within the three previous months, his granddaddy and his great grandmamma had died, leaving our family with much grief and painful loss. From Ben's view, Granddaddy and Granny were in Sunday school, and Jesus was the teacher. The white streak was Jesus writing on the chalkboard. We stood in the parking lot marveling at Jesus's teaching through the eyes of a child. A fresh look at an ordinary occurrence changes everything! Perspective is defined as a particular attitude toward or way of regarding something—a point of view. My view is often skewed by my own notions or feelings at a particular moment in time. But that day in the parking lot, I looked through the eyes of a child with an unfiltered perspective and truly glimpsed what is possible with a fresh look.

As the boys and I forged through their growing up, we daily stumbled upon the need to look at life from the other's perspective. Ben, at four years old, tried to explain the pictures of Matt right after birth—before he was cleaned by the nurses—by deducing that somehow, Matt was covered in mayonnaise. As most parents do before leaving the house, I always asked the boys to try and go to the bathroom first. Ben had become frustrated with my advice and one day blurted out for me to stop "making him be a girl!" Upon further investigation, I realized that Ben thought girls went to the bathroom more than boys, so I was making him be a girl—a different perspective. Matt was always a big kid, but his best friend, on his eleven-year, all-star baseball team, was much smaller than Matt. He was so excited when after a game, he was going to spend the night with his friend. Very late that evening, I received an extremely disturbing call from Matt. He was whispering at the time so as not to wake up the family. My thoughts of why he called ran rampant in my head until I could fully understand his concern. "MOM, I AM STARVING!" I couldn't believe this. Had this family not fed my son? Of course, they fed him! They just fed him food that was in much smaller portions, and food that he perceived to be an unacceptable meal. When I asked him if he told them he was hungry, he emphatically reported they only offered my eleven-year-old granola bars. "Mom, come and get me so I can eat!" Of course, I hung up the phone and left him there, knowing he was not starving and not in danger with this precious family that just had a different perspective on food as Matt did. That became the test for Matt to spend the night—what did they eat?

"You are making a mountain out of a molehill." I never really digested the importance of that saying until I became a parent. You see, that adage is all about perspective. For me, a most challenging part of parenting is keeping a perspective that is helpful to my family. One day, in response to normal happenings with teenage boys in the house, I actually began blubbering. "I feel like Job." It took Ben, much older now but still with fresh perspective, to snap me back into reality with a, "Mom, it's not THAT bad." With the intensity of motherhood, it can only take a second to lose perspective and thus, hamper a good response.

When Ben was just a month or so old, he accidently rolled off the bed. As new parents, we thought our life was over and that we had ruined our child. We scooped him up in a panic and rushed him to the hospital. With no obvious signs of trauma or even a hint of anything wrong, the doctors correctly concluded that this was our first baby and sent us home. We were not wrong when we rushed to the hospital with our baby; we were just new parents reacting out of our limited vision. We needed a realistic perspective.

Matt found himself in trouble over and over for years and years of his young life. I was the first mom in line for pickup every day at John Baker Elementary School, but I was the last mom to leave every day. Why? Because Matt had to be sent back time after time to retrieve something he had left in the classroom. Many times in Guam, Ben and I would scour the neighborhood after school, looking for Matt. Why? Because he forgot to mention he wanted to visit a friend. Matt did not receive credit for his homework time and time again in middle school. Why? Because the homework that he completed the night before wound up in the black hole we called a locker. For these and many more incidents, my perspective was that Matt intentionally disobeyed; and therefore, my response was, you guessed it, punishment. But the reality, as I later understood, was that SOME of Matt's behavior was not born out of disobedience but was a part of his makeup due to attention deficit disorder. I needed a realistic perspective.

We all have a way of seeing the facts or relevant data around us, and then processing them and reacting to them. My problems arise in parenting when I use my natural perspective and then react instead of using God's set of realities from which to react. In parental practice, my reactions are sometimes just "ugly." And I believe that it is because my perspective is sometimes cloudy. I Corinthians 13:11–12 speaks of growth in perspective: "When I was a child, I talked like a child; I thought like a child, I reasoned like a child. When I became a man, I put childish ways behind me. Now we see but a poor reflection as in a mirror; then we shall see face-to-face. Now I know in part; then I shall know fully, even as I am fully known." My perspective, my view of things as I see them, is growing. I am learning and changing. As my perspective grows more in line with Christ in parenting, my response will become more appropriate. My method of learning to react with a more godly perspective is that I must get to know God better. To strengthen my relationship with God is to be a better parent because I will react better when circumstances do arise!

As a child, Matt would emphatically tell us how things were from his view. He would say, "Since I am the youngest, I was the last person to be with Jesus in heaven, so I know what He thinks." In a way, Matt has it right. The last person to be with Jesus, the one who spends time with him, will more likely see things as Jesus sees them. Time spent knowing Jesus will change our daily perspective and our practical responses. I had made my first German chocolate cake for church potluck. It looked terrible. It fell all to pieces and looked more like crumbles of baked flour, coconut, and sticky nuts than a cake. Saddened by my work, I immediately declared that I would never take that to the church potluck. People would expect more from the chaplain's wife! Ben, with a point of view of an eight-year-old boy said, "Mom, its cake! Nobody cares what it looks like as long as it tastes good!" He feared that didn't work, so he hit me with a more heavenly viewpoint. "Mom, remember, God doesn't look at the outside. He just cares about the inside." So with that admonition, I boxed up my cake for church and created a label to put in front of the cake that read, "The Lord does not look at the things man looks at. Man looks at the outward appearance, but the Lord looks at the heart" (1 Sam. 16; 7b). After the potluck, the only thing left of the cake to take home were a few crumbs of coconut. Looking at things from a heavenly perspective changes our responses. Man looked at David and saw a shepherd; God saw a king. I looked at my cake and saw a disaster; Ben saw DESSERT!

Scripture has helped me apply my heart to a more godly perspective many, many times. My boys may affirm, if you ever talk with them, that I am sometimes prone to first respond with a more negative approach when their perspective differed from mine with issues of grades, friend choices, behaviors, incidents that occurred, and the list goes on. But as I learned to check my response to an eternal perspective, I more effectively dealt with the earthly situations. These scriptures are but a few examples that helped me see a greater vision and develop a more eternal mindset as I attempt to parent my two boys. Psalm 112:7 might look like this, "He or she will have no fear of a D coming home on a test (or several) in their junior year of high school. His heart is steadfast, trusting in the Lord." Psalm 46:1–2 may look like this, "God is our refuge and strength, an ever-present help in trouble. Therefore we will not fear though our child is sitting on the sidelines after a hard hit in a football game, or they are carting him off the basketball court after spraining his ankle again." Isaiah 54:10, in the parent version, may read, "Though my child has lied again and his disobeyed again, yet my unfailing love for you will not be shaken, nor my covenant of peace be removed says the Lord, who has compassion on you." All these horrendous things—the mountains being shaken and the hills being removed, the bad grades, the bad news, the letter home from the school about absences you were not aware of, the trouble, the less than affirming teacher conference, the earth being removed or the mountains falling into the heart of the sea, the concussions and black eyes and broken bones—may happen. But remembering who God is and what He is doing creates a new perspective on the most disastrous events. Most of the time, I have realized that what I thought was disaster was just dessert.

It might be my age, but I am waking up in the middle of the night fairly regularly. During the night when it is dark and everyone else is asleep, I do my best thinking and my worst thinking. Greg and the boys hate to see me coming the next morning because I interrogate them concerning all the bad things I conjured up during the dark hours I was awake. Things can seem so big and so worrisome to me in the night, but when I recall them out loud to my family the next day in the light of day, somehow, those things diminish in size and seem somewhat insignificant. In the same way, having God's light and His thoughts, His view on a situation changes our scenarios from overwhelming to very manageable and sometimes insignificant. I can't see to parent in the dark, and the perspective of the world offers us much darkness. But as the light of Christ shines, we can see. "You are my lamp O Lord; the Lord turns my darkness into light" (2 Sam. 22:29). "Your word is a lamp to my feet and a light to my path" (Ps. 119:105). "I will bring the blind by a way that they don't know. I will lead them in paths that they don't know. I will make darkness light before them and crooked places straight, I will do these things and I will not forsake them" (Isa. 42:16). "There will be no more night. They will not need the light of a lamp or the light of the sun, for the Lord God will give them light and they will reign forever and ever" (Rev. 22:5).

We were moving from Turkey where the boys shared a room with two twin beds, to Albuquerque where they would now have their own rooms and big beds all by themselves. Ben was thrilled, but Matt was less than enthusiastic. I could not understand why he was not excited about this new arrangement. I keep telling him that he was even getting his papa's old bedroom suite and bed. The boys went to their first day of their new school in Albuquerque, and I did as I always had, quickly unpacked their rooms first so they could feel at home wherever we were. Finally, the job was done, the boys came home to their new individual rooms, and then it appeared— the joy and excitement from Matt that I was hoping for. I wondered why the change suddenly when he was able to see his room. Then he exclaimed, "Mama, this isn't an old bed! This is great!" I further understood that old to Matt meant rusty and ugly. With a fresh understanding, Matt saw not rusty and ugly, but the cherished antique that was his new bed!

Eyes closed and head bobbing, Greg and I laughed as our toddler almost fell asleep at dinner one night. But his older and wiser brother had a different take on the situation instructing us, "He's not asleep. He's just praising the Lord with his eyes closed." The words shared from the view of a four-year-old often silenced our laughter and replaced our judgment with a truly new perspective.

Ouch! Parenting Can Be Hazardous to Your Health

God warned us in Genesis that "with pain we would give birth to children" (3:16). That is definitely true, but I do not remember Him warning us that with the rearing of children, we would have pain. But that is also a certainty. We hurt when our children are battered by external circumstances, we hurt when changes come and we feel powerless to protect or help, and we hurt when our children make atrocious choices which result in consequences we have to watch them suffer. Wow! I know this chapter has started out a bit gloomy, but please don't skip it! Let's trust for a moment that every cloud does have a silver lining. I believe that is biblical. Isaiah 53:11a encourages us: "After the suffering of his soul, he will see the light of life and be satisfied."

"It's not fair!" Matt, my second born, asserted. This phrase could have been the first three words he put together in a sentence. With pouty lips, crossed arms, and furrowed brow, he declared it over and over in almost every situation where things didn't go his way. I would always agree. "It may not be fair, but so much about life isn't fair." Maybe this concept was too much for a young boy to grasp; maybe it was too much for a mom of a young boy to grasp. I found myself with the same pouty lips and arms crossed but with an added pain in my chest many times. Times when the boys got physically hurt and they just wanted me to make it better. Times when they came home from school hurt after someone had made fun of them. Times when they were waiting to be put in the game but their names weren't called. Yes, that lump in my throat was the pain of parenting; and with everything in me, I wanted to scream, "It's not fair!"

Since we moved every two to three years, the boys were always each other's best friend. Because Matt was always big for his age, he mostly played with Ben and his friends. I never realized how tough the separation of these two buddies would be until we moved to Colorado, and Ben went to high school and Matt stayed in middle school. Matt played school basketball, club basketball, baseball, and middle school football, and had many "friends" who were really just acquaintances. Downcast and with those same pouty cheeks and lips, just a big larger version, Matt finally confided in me that he was never invited to any of the birthday parties of his teammates. He surmised that he just didn't fit in. Several years later, as the other kids grew, one of these same teammates told Matt, "We just didn't get you. We didn't understand you." I watched Matt's pain. I shared his pain. I couldn't change his pain. We walked through it.

I had been a sports mom since the boys began playing organized ball at two years old. Yes—hard core! So much of my pain had come from the world of sports. Believe me—it had a lot to offer. (The parents are ridiculous, but that's another book.) From Little League baseball to Pop Warner football to Upward Basketball, the early years of the boys' competition afforded us small aches, but nothing could prepare me for late-teen years when competition for college scholarships made it all very real. Matt had been invited to Utah to throw (he was a pitcher) in a showcase for a chance to move on to compete for a spot on a USA baseball team. He had thrown seven innings and had done so well that his coaches had assured him that his name would be called to move on to the next round of competition. The stadium at Brigham Young University was filled with baseball players and parents eagerly awaiting the results of the competition. I was sitting alone but around hundreds of anxious, fidgety parents. Matt was with his team. I couldn't wait to hear his name called and to see him stand alongside the other players whose talents were being celebrated. Name after name was called; my chest grew tighter and tighter until the announcer had concluded with the last name, and it was not Matt. What happened? I was not prepared for the pain and hurt that literally took my breath away. Matt was hurt, and there was nothing I could do but share his pain. I couldn't change his pain. We walked through it.

His blood ran orange for many days, so did his hair and everyday his clothing. Matt was a Clemson fan from the day he knew about Clemson. Of course, it did help that during the formative times of picking teams, his dad, who pulled for Carolina (South Carolina), was deployed. Matt's dream was to play baseball for Clemson. He practiced and worked hard with that goal in mind. We had been corresponding with the recruiting coach at Clemson for a while, so the summer between his junior and senior year of high school, Matt was invited to try out for the coaches. Although we were from South Carolina, to these coaches, he was some kid from New Mexico. The tryout was a joke—and Matt did poorly. The coaches rudely dismissed his talent, and in one minute, the whole of my son's dreams burst and I couldn't do a thing! His blood changed colors that day. It still hurts. With all the externals that hurt our children, I have learned that I can't do anything to solve it, but I will and do hurt with them. It doesn't change the pain, but we walk through it together.

The boys grew quickly, and their legs often hurt due to this growth. These growing pains were a result of change in their physical stature; but we also had many growing pains that were a result of change in our relationship, dependencies, and roles. I used to hear from my boys, "Mama, you are the only girl for me." How times have changed! Sometimes, I felt the pain because of my need to keep things just as they were. But this pain I was feeling was just the beginning, and I knew that I would have to realize it was not about me. The pains we experience because of our changing roles are mostly obscure to our children. Their behaviors through these life stages are normal—they should happen—but we grieve the change anyway. The amount of time we get to spend with our children changes as they get older, drive, acquire more friends, and do various activities outside the family. When they begin sharing more feelings with a girlfriend rather than a mom or dad, it gives us as parents both happiness for them mixed with a twinge of ache for us. But these are natural and normal to the growth process, so they are more easily overcome than some other hurts. Greg and I couldn't stop and wouldn't want to stop these changes because we expect and celebrate them, so we go through the "ouch" of them together.

From babies to toddlers to children to preteen to teenager to young adult, we are still their parents. But the struggle to determine what that means and how that works out in relationship is sometimes painful during the transition. They need you; they don't need you. They want your help; they don't want your help. It's like pulling peddles off a forget-me-not and wondering where you will land. And by the way, your status could change again tomorrow. I was pretty fortunate in that throughout middle school and even high school, my boys chose to be seen with me, hug me, wanted to talk with me, embraced doing things with the family, and mostly listened to me. The pain came for me when they left for college. Not necessarily because we were empty nesters and I missed their presence, although I did. But when my seventeen-year-old sons left home for college (two years apart), they really left home and moved all the way across the country. They both had a strong desire to prove responsibility, to be the man, to enter this task alone, to encounter this big change in their life without our counsel and without a strong commitment to our relationship through communication. Now THAT hurt!

The letting-go period was too abrupt. I grieved the loss of the emotional tie that we had had, but I knew they had to maneuver the time between boy and man in their own way. So as we did again what we did when they were infants, we gave them to the Lord, our pain and all. Each one of them, in their own way, eventually realized the separation between us that had been caused by an "I'll do it alone and do it my way" attitude; and soon enough, they each came back emotionally. In dealing with the consequences of their behavior, the boys learned that the home that was once a shelter where they had learned and grown and enjoyed fellowship had become a refuge to where they could return and learn and grow and fellowship again. "He who fears the Lord has a secure fortress, and for his children it will be a refuge" (Prov. 14:26) Pain comes and pain goes, and we walk through it together.

Pain and hurt in parenting come many times because we have no control over the choices our children make. As our control lessens, their ability to make decisions without us increases; and often, the consequences of those decisions cause pain. We lived in Colorado and had gone to Steamboat Springs for a baseball tournament for Matt. The team, plus Ben, decided to float down the river. It was a sunny day, but cool, so Ben dismissed our admonition to wear a T-shirt or to put on sunscreen. As they develop, sometimes, they act with maturity and thus suffer little consequences; but sometimes, they act immaturely and suffer great consequences. We picked up Ben and Matt at the end of the float. Ben did not immediately face the repercussions of his decision, but as Greg and I looked at him, we knew it was coming and did not have to say a word. That night, he moaned and groaned like a woman in travail, spouting, "I'm gonna die!"

Watching Ben's pain after getting sunburned was painful for us just because we had to hear him complain constantly. While this was a small thing, there are times when the choices that our growing children make cause us tremendous pain. We hate to see them have to go through the pain of consequences especially when they knew and we knew what could happen. Yet because of sin—arrogance of heart—they choose against what they know, against what they have been taught, against our advice—they choose. That hurts not only them but us as their parents, who throughout their lives, have attempted to shield them from pain. Our pain is enhanced by the many questions that race through our minds as to what we could have done differently. What was our culpability in this? And the guilt that Satan offers when we don't have the answers.

Your pain in parenting may be very different from mine. Many parents suffer because their children suffer physical pain. Others grieve due to more external circumstances inflicted upon their children, yet other parents have intense pain caused by the indiscretions of their children. Be assured that if you are a parent, at some point, you will experience pain because you have children. Thankfully, we have a God who understands, and has grieved and felt pain over his children. "The Lord was grieved that He had made man on the earth and His heart was filled with pain" (Gen. 6:6). "Yet they rebelled and grieved His Holy Spirit" (Isa. 63:10a). We may feel very dramatic sometimes like the verse in Lamentations: "This is why I weep and my eyes overflow with tears. No one is near to comfort me and no one is near to restore my spirit. My children are destitute because the enemy has prevailed" (1:16). However, we as believing parents know this may be our feeling, but it is not our truth. Our God is one who is acquainted with grief. Isaiah 53:3a says, "He was despised and rejected by men, a man of sorrows, and familiar with suffering." Because He is the perfect parent who has experienced pain and understands our pain, we can be comforted by Him. Psalm 34:18 reminds us, "The Lord is close to the brokenhearted and saves those who are crushed in spirit." And Isaiah emphasizes, "The Lord comforts his people and will have compassion on his afflicted ones."

So where in the world is the silver lining I talked about when I asked you to not skip this chapter? It was a Saturday morning and the boys were filing out of the car for the Little League baseball game they were playing in about an hour. Ben got out of the car with bad attitude all over his being, and although he couldn't shake it off himself, it splattered all over us. Needless to say, the morning started badly. The game was going well. Ben was at shortstop, and Matt was at first base. Then a hard-hit ball took a bad bounce right in front of Ben, hitting him in the cheekbone and eye area, and then bouncing into our second baseman's glove for the out. Which was very important. Many parents beat me onto the field, as I was always told by the boys NOT to EVER go running out on the field. But Ben was on the ground and his eye had swollen shut, so it was an appropriate occasion to charge the field. We rushed him to the hospital while Matt, who also wanted to go, was instructed by the coach to get back to first base. After all, this Little League game was of utmost importance. When Ben realized he wasn't blind—he opened his eye—and the doctor told him the only thing he would suffer was the pain and a lasting black eye, we finally could breathe a sigh of relief.

However, the pain was useful to Ben. He thought through the events prior to the game and recalled that he had been quite ugly to his family just before getting out of the car before the game. He asked me if God did this to teach him a lesson. I advised him that God did NOT cause his pain, but sometimes, He would allow us to go through pain to help us and to teach us. Ben did get back out on the baseball field the next game, but he never left the van without asking, "Did I do anything to hurt y'all? Are we okay?" In other words, he learned from his pain.

Using our pain for good is the silver lining. We can comfort others as we have been comforted (2 Cor. 1:3–4). We will grow in patience, endurance, and character (Rom. 5:3). A silver lining to our pain comes when we become more conscious of God as expressed in 1 Peter 2:19: "For it is commendable if a man bear up under the pain of unjust suffering because he is conscious of God." A silver lining to our pain is the restoration God brings. "And the God of all grace, who called you to his eternal glory in Christ, after you have suffered a little while, will himself restore you and make you strong, firm and steadfast" (1 Pet. 5:10).

In a devotional by Oswald Chambers, *My Utmost for His Highest*, he says, "In the Bible, clouds are always connected with God. Clouds are those sorrows, sufferings, or providences, within or without our personal lives, which seem to dispute the rule of God. It is by these very clouds that the Spirit of God is teaching us how to walk by faith. If there were no cloud, we should have no faith." At twenty years old, Matt came to a crossroads in his life. For several years in college, he had believed the lie that he was not smart enough and could never pass the classes that were very challenging to him—math! The problem had become so grave that if he did not pass the math class he was taking, he would be kicked out of a second school and would no longer be able to play college baseball. Incapacitated to change any of Matt's circumstances, I grieved and hurt. Matt had heard all the encouragements and knew of all the helps available, yet he was paralyzed by fear; so I watched in pain. With this massive cloud, I could only cry out to God and enlist every person I knew on my Facebook, Sunday school class, family, PWOC, and neighborhood to PRAY. When I didn't know what to say in my pain, I knew whose name to say, JESUS.

Matt entered the math final with a failing grade, but he made an 85 on the cumulative final and passed the class! Days later, Matt explained that in his desperation, he also had cried out to God and said, "I want to play baseball. If you want me to play baseball, I need help. I am going to do everything I know how to do to study and get help to pass this test. Please, you help me, and I will be satisfied with what you do as long as I do my best." Matt concluded with, "Mama, I finally BELIEVE GOD!" I would never have chosen the pain or the cloud in order for Matt to finally believe God in his life but what a silver lining.

> "Trust in the Lord with all your heart and lean not on your own understanding, acknowledge him in all your ways, and he will make your paths straight" (Prov. 3:5–6).

> "And we know that in all things God works for the good of those who love him, who have been called according to his purpose" (Rom. 8:28).

> "I am still confident of this; I will see the goodness of the Lord in the land of the living. Wait for the Lord, be strong and take heart and wait for the Lord" (Ps. 27:13–14).

Super Mom

While writing in my journal, I realized a disturbing trend forming. I was asking the Lord to help me be strong for Ben, Matt, and Greg. I felt that was kind of sad. Instead of praying for each of them to be strong with God, I was praying that I could be strong for them. Wow! I have become more than I needed to be, more than I should be. I had become Super Mom and Super Wife! Let me explain further, and if this is you, keep reading.

We were living in Turkey in the middle of the longest Turkish union labor strike in history. Because we were living on a Turkish Air Force base, any business that employed a Turkish worker was closed until the strike was over. We were also not allowed to leave the base during the duration of the strike. Because of the strike rules, the commissary (the military grocery store) and the shopette (the military version of a 7-Eleven) were closed, so there was no place to buy American food. In order to solve this problem for the military families stationed at Incirlik Air Base, the adults were loaded on buses with blacked-out windows and escorted by armed guards to a Turkish grocery store an hour away. We were only allowed to get enough food that could be put in a backpack so that when we were let off at an undisclosed location on base, the strikers would only see people with backpacks and not question us. As a first grader, the only thing Ben would eat for lunch was a peanut butter and jelly sandwich. So every morning, faithfully, I would make his sandwich. Thankfully, I had a large jar of American jelly because having looked at the Turkish jelly, I realized it was runny and would not have passed the Ben test to make an appropriate peanut butter and jelly sandwich. One morning after making his sandwich, I put the jelly back in the door rack of the refrigerator. When I began to shut the refrigerator door, the bar holding the jelly in place broke; the jelly jar fell to the floor, broke, and grape jelly was all over my marble floor! I fell prostrate on the floor going after the jelly, screaming and crying. Ben didn't understand. "Mom, it's okay. My sandwich is already made." But he didn't see the future like I did, and tomorrow, there could be no sandwich without MY provision. So with my best Scarlet O'Hara indignation, I got off the floor and announced that as God as my witness, I would get him some American jelly! Because I am mom, that was what I did. I went from house to house begging for jelly. See, that is my job as a mom, right? I am his provider.

The same year that I heroically secured the jelly for my son, another more pressing situation arose. I was entering a building on base to renew my Turkish resident permit along with my pre-kindergarten son Matt, when loud sirens began booming all over the base. The military members raced out of the building in droves as I was entering. I stopped an airman to inquire about the frantic activity. He very politely answered that a scud missile had been launched in our direction, and they were donning their gas masks in preparation for the event. Oh! Very aware of the fact that my son and I had zero equipment to put on, I less than politely asked back, "Well, what are we supposed to do?" Having never considered the question, the airman hemmed and hawed around and said, "I guess you can stay in here."

Not me! With sirens blaring and people scattering to get off the streets, Matt and I and another chaplain's wife who was with us headed straight for the elementary school on base where our other children were. We slid in the door as one of the last persons to get in before the doors were shut and all were locked down. The children, all playing in the gym with some parents and other siblings watching along, were oblivious to the outside terror. But I was there. I was there to protect my child. What? I am not sure how I thought I was going to protect them from a missile, for heaven sake, but I was there! I am a mom, and that's what I do! As we waited and waited for something to happen, my friend offered a more excellent word, "It's a good day to know Jesus!"

So this Super Mom is a provider, protector, and what about medical helper? When Ben was about four, he and my daddy were playing hide and seek as Greg and I were packing up the car to head back home after a time of visiting. Ben decided to hide under the propped-up boat motor. When he was found, he jumped up and gashed his head wide open. With blood gushing profusely down his head all over his face, my daddy grabbed him up and ran him to the house to find us. Upon seeing him, I panicked! Greg calmly got a towel to stop the bleeding and put him in the car to our doctor friend in town, you guessed it—the gynecologist! He put butterfly stitches on Ben's head, and all was well. But having relinquished my Super Mom status in the medical accident department, I had to reboot my efforts elsewhere.

Of course, I became all and more that my boys needed. I was chief homework checker and caller outer. My son was home from college the other day and had a test coming up the next week. I asked if there was something I could call out in preparation for his test. He commented that he was okay and then just smiled and said, "Mom, I know you just miss calling things out." Indignantly, I thought, *Are you kidding? This is not about ME. I just was helping YOU!*

I attended every baseball, basketball, and football game cheering loudly and with great fervor, and sometimes, to the boys' dismay. When the boys became older, my Super Mom support was always appreciated, but my Super Mom cheering was somewhat altered. Ben suggested that I not yell for him to "be a wall" as he was catching baseball behind the plate, and Matt suggested that I not yell that he "just throw strikes" while pitching. Apparently, both of the technical instructions offered needed not to be said and certainly not stated loudly by their mom!

As prayer warriors go, I was the one agonizing many days and nights and in many locations. The school year afforded me many opportunities to get on my knees. Tests, projects, homework assignments were covered. Special prayers were offered before, during, and after every teacher conference. Not sure if I or Matt offered more prayers during that time. Many nights, I would be awakened by a nagging need to pray about a school issue; and the next morning, a particular boy would be awakened by a nagging—well, you get it, Super Mom—in order to rehearse the concerns I dwelt on during the night.

I am and was the provider of emotional support, physical support, and all other support that I could conjure and more. All of the things that I did and do as a Super Mom were and are well intentioned and good. But then, I heaped more emotional strain on myself as I began to realize that I only have two children and others around me have four, six, and even some we have known with nine or more. I don't make my own bread, I don't home school, so what else must I do to prove that I am Super Mom? After all, Psalm 127:3–5 says, "Sons are a heritage from the Lord, children a reward from him. Like arrows in the hands of a warrior are sons born in one's youth. Blessed is the man whose quiver is full of them." I felt like everybody else's quiver, a case for storing arrows, was better because they had more children. So I doubted myself until I realized that God had just given me a smaller quiver, and it was full! Since it was full, I could again put all my energy into caring for my little arrows once again.

The stress of trying to be this Super Mom, shoulder all the needs of those in my quiver, and doing so many times with a deployed spouse got the best of me one day, okay, many days. But on this day in particular, the only thing that spared me from decking a lady at church was the fact that I was the Wing Chaplain's Wife, and that kind of behavior is frowned upon. She, being a mom of young children, commented to me that since my boys were seventeen and nineteen, this deployment should be very easy. Gritting my teeth, but with very little hesitation, I lectured her on child development issues and the problems that having teenage boys incur. I described the lack of control that I now had over their behavior, their choices, and their friends, and how I sometimes desired the physical work of parenting young children to that of the strenuous emotional work I was now doing. With that, she sheepishly walked away, and I was left feeling drained, lacking something and not feeling much like a super hero.

What did I need? Certainly not a pedicure. I can't imagine spending money for having someone paint my toenails, although so many of my friends love this. I love to get massages, but I get scared

I will fall asleep and not enjoy it completely; and when it is over, it's over. I could go buy a piece of jewelry. That is a true weakness. I like jewelry, and I justify having several—lots—of it because the Bible speaks of all the jewels that will be in heaven. So really, I am just practicing a bit of heaven. No, that is not what I need either. When the boys were toddlers, we were living at Moody Air Force Base in Valdosta, Georgia. We met Greg for lunch at Burger King on base. After lunch, I loaded the boys up in the BX (Base Exchange) buggy (shopping cart) and headed off to do some shopping. Matt was in the front of the buggy and Ben was in the big part with all of the items we were buying. At the end of our BX excursion, and without warning, Matt turned his head around toward Ben and threw up his Burger King lunch all over Ben's head and the merchandise we were going to buy. Ben stood up covered in Matt's used lunch and exclaimed, "GET THIS KID AWAY FROM ME!" I took Ben and Matt out of the buggy and, with the blessing of the BX workers, left the unbought merchandise and Matt's mess in the middle of the BX and went home.

Parenting is messy, and trying to be a super mom is very messy. My tired and drained super hero body often wanted to shout, "Get these kids away from me!" But in those times of weakness, I relinquished my cape to a real super hero and quieted myself to the words of one of my favorite songs by Twila Paris:

> Lately, I've been winning battles left and right,
> But even winners can get wounded in the fight,
> People say that I'm amazing, strong beyond my years,
> But they don't see inside of me, I'm hiding all the tears.
> They don't know that I go running home when I fall down,
> They don't know who picks me up when no one is around,
> I drop my sword and cry for just a while,
> Cause deep inside this armor, the Warrior is a Child.

So that's what I did, and that's what I do. I can't shoulder the Super Mom duties without running home to my Super Hero, my heavenly Father. I realize I don't have to be a Super Mom. God does not want me to be a Super Mom. He wants me to rely on Him! He is my provider, He is my strength, and He is my protector—the source of my emotional, physical, and mental stability. He is my peace and my rest, and I run home to Him. I read his word for me where he says, "Cast all your care on him, because he cares for you" (1 Pet.5:7); and in Matthew 11:28–30, Jesus says, "Come to me all you who are weary and burdened, and I will give you rest, Take my yoke upon you and learn from me, for I am gentle and humble in heart and you will find rest for your souls. For my yoke is easy and my burden is light." I sit with Him and pray as I tell Him all about my troubles as the psalmist suggests. As I write: my load is lessoned and my journals are full (and Greg fears our weight allowance for our military move will be maxed out).

Whenever I still sometimes struggle with trying to be everything for my boys, or young men, I drop my sword and my Super Mom façade, and run home where I rest, regroup, and see the truth of the battle. I don't have to be their everything. I don't want to be their everything. I just want to point them to my everything!

All You

Matt has a game that he has played for years now. It began when he saw me lying down on the bed or floor or couch, wherever I happened to be reclining. He would flop on me with all his weight, hold his arms out as if flying, and without touching anything, trying hard not to lose his balance and bombastically exclaimed, "All you! All you! It's all on you!" He had managed to put all his weight on me. When he was little, this was such a cute little game that I also loved to play. Many times, I perched on the floor in front of him on purpose just so he would pounce on me and begin our ritual with him trying to balance all his weight on me while we laughed and loved. But as he grew, he still wanted to play the game, which for me became less and less fun. After all, Matt was now six foot five and one-half inches tall, and weighs about two hundred and fifty pounds! I definitely couldn't play the game on the floor anymore! But there are times when my sweet large son wants to play, so he tosses me to the bed and, yes, squashes me while victoriously proclaiming, "All you! All you! It's all on you!"

It was a game. It was a challenge. Could he actually balance all his weight on me? How long could I hold up under his weight? The game, easy at first, became more difficult as Matt grew because the burden of carrying his weight grew, and I could not carry his weight very long. While I for sure needed to stop playing this game with Matt, for obvious reasons, it occurred to me that I MUST play this game with God. So many times while parenting, I carried a huge load. Every parent carries the loads of physically watching over the children, providing for their every need, ensuring their security, promoting their growth (in every area), nurturing their heart toward God, and the list goes on and on. So God tells us to play the game with Him. Put all our weight on Him. Trust that He can sustain all our weight, and we freely and triumphantly profess, "All you! All you! It's all on you, God!" Unlike me who begins to quiver under the weight of my very large son, our weight is never a burden to God. Unlike me who has a time limit for the game, God is willing and able to carry us for as long as we are willing to place our weight on Him.

"Officially the worst deployment ever!" I shouted while stuck in a hotel room in South Carolina alone for days, waiting for flood-waters to subside. I had already visited with my son and his fiancé, and now was trying to visit my mama and daddy who were stuck in their house due to floodwaters blocking all the roads into their town. Greg had already been gone five months but had seven more to go! Did I declare this the worst deployment ever because it was the longest? Or was it because with the boys both in college, I was alone? Or because it seemed that everyone in my family was having huge issues during this deployment and I was helpless to control any of them? Or was it because on top of everything else, I had a physical issue for which there was no cure, and stress made it worse? I began to think that I longed for the days when deployments seemed easier. But then I realized this was not the first time I had declared, "Officially the worst deployment ever!" As I lay on the bed in that hotel room, I also remembered I had to flop on Jesus with all my weight as I had done in every other deployment or extended time when Greg was away for the military. It didn't matter if the deployment was one month, five months, or twelve months; in each one, the weight seemed heavy. All the weight of raising the boys, tending the house, keeping the family afloat during the times of singular parenting was on ME. But I wasn't alone, so I began to learn to flop on Jesus, let Him hold the weight, all the weight, for the whole time.

The boys were two and four at the time of Greg's very first extended military deployment. I had determined in my heart to be the BEST dad and mom to the boys and to do whatever it took to make this deployment painless and without incident. We started off great with projects of colored sand in jars to make little deserts like where Daddy was living. Although after teaching about deserts, I did have to convince the boys that Dad did not go over there to catch them a camel. We made a chain of construction paper links with just the right amount of days until Daddy came home, and every night, the boys took a link and made paper confetti. As we threw the confetti up in the air, we danced and sang, "Another day down till Daddy comes home." The chain grew shorter so the boys could see when Daddy was coming home, but my resolve began to fade as I had to add paper chain links at night when the boys were asleep as news that Daddy's arrival home would not be as first planned.

The determination to be the best dad a mom could be, led me to the baseball closet to get the equipment that Greg and the boys used for their boys day outing. I had the bag, the gloves, the helmet, and the bats, and of course, the Big League Chew. Heading out the door with my baseball cap on and two very small boys in tow, Ben timidly asked, "Mom, can we just go to the park?" Confused, I questioned, "But why, Ben? This is what Daddy does. Don't you want to play baseball? We are going to have fun just like on boy's day!" Trying not to look at me in the eyes when he answered, he replied, "Mama, can we just go to the park? You don't throw the ball so good." I wasn't sure whether to laugh, cry, or be offended. But I did what Ben needed—put the equipment back, ran to the park, and laughed and played. That night, when alone, I did cry; and I put my weight on Jesus. I hated that their daddy was not there. I cried that it wasn't fair. These boys needed their daddy, and I couldn't be that for them. Jesus carried my weight that night and comforted me as He reminded me just to be ME for them—be their mom! That God, their heavenly Father, loved my boys more than I could, and He was right there. All you, God.

So my quest to be just ME—to be the PERFECT MOM—began. I had never made a homemade pizza, so I thought this would be a great opportunity to excel and show the boys how great I could be. I loaded the pizza with enough ground beef, sausage, and pepperoni that would surely impress my little carnivores. Sadly, when it came out of the oven, the crust was soggy, dripping with grease, and not at all like I had imagined. I served it up, and once again, Ben, with those same inquiring eyes, suggested, "Hey, Mom, does that man who brought pizzas to the door still do that? Can we just call him?" Looking at that disgusting mess, I tossed it in the trash and, to the boys' great joy, called the pizza man. I learned that night I could be Mom, but sometimes, it looked different from what I had envisioned—not perfect. I had been able to provide for my boys to adjust my thinking and to grow; so at night, when the boys were asleep, I whispered, "Thanks, God—ALL you."

By the end of every day, I was physically and mentally exhausted that first deployment when the boys were so young. Nevertheless, God showed up to carry my weight every time, often through people from church, volunteer babysitters, or surprise gifts of free massages. Because we were assigned two remotes to Turkey and Guam as a family, Greg wasn't tasked for another long deployment until we were stationed at the Air Force Academy. The boys were in middle school, so I assumed this deployment would be easily managed. The left turn blinker went out in the car, so I only made right turns. Hey, I've got this managed. The hot water heater started spewing water all over the floor in the basement, so I ran outside, screaming my problem from neighbor to neighbor until one told me to first shut off the water. What? Where was that? I found the water shutoff—I am very knowledgeable now—and bought a new hot water heater. I had this deployment managed.

Until I had an eighth-grade boy baseball player issue for which I was not at all equipped to handle, and I realized that objects were easy to take care of, but my children required much more. During the introductions of the all-star team in front of all the Little League teams and parents, Matt was announced to be the "hope" of our Little League all-star team, making it to the Little League World Series with his pitching. That's a pretty tall order for any twelve-year-old but especially one that was carrying an extra weight of a deployed dad—who by the way, was his baseball mentor in every way. I will save you and Matt the gory details and just say that Matt did not pitch well, the coach did not coach well, the team did not play well, and we did not even make it out of district. My heart was heavy, and I had no words for my son who had once believed that HE could carry his team. God, how could I carry Matt when I was so disappointed too? The final ceremony of the season came, and Greg had sent the team an American flag that had been flown over Iraq. I saw Matt lead his team as they all hoisted the flag up the pole, put their hands over their hearts, and pledged allegiance to the flag. At that moment, my twelve-year-old son knew there was something greater than a Little League game for which to fight, and he honored his dad and led his team. God carried my weight, all my weight that day.

Just because God can, and just because He wants to show us above and beyond how He desires to carry our weight, He brought my parents to visit. My devastated eighth-grade baseball player became an exuberant carefree boy who, alongside his papa, counted prong-horn sheep as we drove through Colorado and Wyoming to finally end up at Yellowstone National Park. God many times brought other people to carry me, and to carry my boys.

I had just finished teaching my Tuesday-morning Bible study and was sitting in the car when I received a call from Greg who uncharacteristically was stuttering and fumbling his words badly. I finally encouraged him, then loudly and emphatically asked him, then I screamed, "What is wrong?"

To give context to his answer, I must tell you that Ben, our oldest, was a senior in high school, it was November, we had signed a senior wavier that said we would not move while we had a senior, and we were told that we would get to move to Florida in the sum-mer. Greg's trembling answer was, "I have an assignment." He had just been given a short-notice assignment to be the Wing Chaplain at Cannon Air Force Base in Clovis, New Mexico, with a report date around January 14. Forget the senior wavier, forget Greg being around for Ben's senior baseball season, and forget Florida! This heavy weight that had just been thrust upon me seemed much more than the game of a 6'5", 250-pound kid throwing me to the ground and falling on me with all his weight. As I sat in the car, all the questions came: how will Ben take this? How can we afford two households? How can I sell the house alone? Clovis—not Florida? I sat for a few more minutes and began to sing first in my heart and then out loud as the Spirit of God reminded me:

> "There is no problem too big God cannot solve
> it. There is no mountain too tall He cannot move

it, and there is no storm too dark God cannot calm it. There is no sorrow too deep He cannot soothe it. If He carried the weight of the world upon His shoulders, I know, my brother, that He will carry you. And if He carried the weight of the world upon His shoulders, I know, my sister, that He will carry you. He said, 'Come unto me all who are weary and I will give you rest'" (Lyrics by Scott Wesley Brown).

God was faithful as I laid all my weight on Him that day and each day of the six months after. Greg was able to live at the Associational Missionary Office Building at no cost. My Sunday school class came out in droves one Saturday and moved all unnecessary furniture and household items to a storage unit so I could appropriately arrange the house for real-estate showings. The drive to Clovis was only six hours, so Greg was able to see much of Ben's phenomenal senior baseball season. Greg's ministry at Cannon was one of the most fulfilling of his career so far. Even as I spent days on my hands and knees, cleaning and vacuuming what seemed like thousands of stairs for surprise house showings, I repeated over and over this verse, "I remain confident in this: I will see the goodness of the Lord in the land of the living" (Ps. 27:13). And I did! God sold our house in His perfect timing! We were able to close on the house and all move to Clovis as soon as Ben graduated. All YOU!

Every day, we all have the need to put all our weight on God, but sometimes I must admit that when Greg is around, I tend to rely on him as my strength. God does use people to be our strength, but often, He reminds me of this verse when I hear the word "deployment" again. "Indeed in our hearts we felt the sentence of death. But this happened that we might not rely on ourselves but on God, who raises the dead" (2 Cor. 1:9). I believe God also allows these deployments in my life at certain times where I am becoming a bit too cocky in my ability to hold my own weight. While still living in Clovis, I knew Greg had a deployment coming up in August; but after all, Matt was now a senior in high school, and Ben had come home after changing colleges to regroup and find a college that suited his needs for ROTC. So I surely could handle life with two almost-grown men—guys—in reality, boys! The boys grew up being best friends, and their disagreements were always pretty mild. But on this particular day, a seemingly innocuous disagreement between these very large and strong males resulted in anger, red faces, and lots of chest bowing. So with my 5'8" self, I jumped between this pair who, on this day, were not prepared to be my strength. They separated—one going for a drive—then eventually coming back to talk through the issues.

I couldn't put my weight on my boys that day; but on other days during this deployment, these boys, who were growing into men, became for me a support given straight from God. We were renting our house in town instead of living on base so Matt could be close to the school. As usual, we were caring for the yard: mowing, raking, and weeding the sidewalks as well as around flowerbeds as if we owned the house. After having lived in the neighborhood for two years without one neighbor introducing themselves to us, one day, while Greg was deployed, I received a letter from a neighbor. But as I read through it, I cried, I got hurt, I became angry, and then Ben took over for me. The anonymous letter stated that the neighborhood association had gotten together to discuss how our lack of trimming our shrubs and cutting down of dead trees was hurting the value of their homes. They also said that sometimes, they understood that military families did not care for property as they should. WOW! Welcome to the neighborhood! Ben consoled me and made me laugh as we mounted our defense and headed next door, to the "unknown" author of the letter. Our detective skills enabled us to surmise who wrote the letter. As we stumbled over the large rock plaque on his front porch that read, "As for me and my house, we will serve the Lord," I couldn't help but laugh. But that rock helped turn the angry words that I had prepared into babbling tearful words that went something like this, "Hello, I am Kathy. I live next door to you. I received your letter. My husband is deployed. We are renting, and we take care of the yard, except what the owner is responsible for." Cry...cry...cry. We left. The old man was nearly speechless, not expecting a blubbering lady and her large college-aged son as back up to come calling. Ben, the quiet, supportive type who was ready for a brawl affirmed quite humorously, "Well, Mom, we really told him!"

For our twenty-fifth wedding anniversary, I always imagined a great, big, fun celebration or party commemorating our love and marriage. Then I realized I had boys who I was not sure even knew when our anniversary was. But of course, on this anniversary, our twenty-fifth, the boys were off the hook with the party because Greg was deployed. My heart was heavy, and I was feeling sorry for myself when my seventeen-year-old son Matt burst in the door insisting we Skype Dad. He had gone to Wal-Mart and come back with twenty-four cupcakes! (What happened to the last cupcake is still a mystery.) He took pictures of me and Greg on the computer screen, and we had a celebration of our twenty-five years of marriage! With God using my teenage son to carry me at that moment, I would not have exchanged those precious cupcakes minus that one lost (or eaten) for a big, extravagant party! God is sometimes just beside me, like Ben being a silent support and encouraging me to speak up. God is sometimes like Matt, who brings surprise cupcakes to celebrate when I am heavy of heart. But, as always, All You God

Back to today, the deployment at hand, now seven months down and five to go, but was it really the worst deployment ever? I had learned many lessons. Matt even reminded me of something he had actually heard from me. "Mom, you have always told me that I need to ask for help. So why don't you?" Psalm 54:4 says, "Surely God is my help, the Lord is the one who sustains me." So as I have asked, and even when I didn't ask, God was my help; and He sent me help in many forms. When at night, alone, my thoughts seemed to grow worse, God sent me peace and rest as I listened to His words through music. I was thrilled when countless church people told me they were praying for Greg, but secretly, I wanted to say, "Would you pray for me?" I stopped the secret desires, and I asked out loud. I asked for prayer for me too, and people prayed—for me! I learned to ask for help this deployment, so it must not be the worst.

I hate to drive long distances. I have always been a superb navigator and a short-relief driver on our long trips. While my husband excelled at long-distance driving, I would do anything to keep him occupied and thus maintain my sidecar status. I would read him the newspaper, play word power games in Reader's Digest, and listen to his choice of radio options. But now, my driver was deployed; and due to family situations in South Carolina that required me to have my car, I needed to drive from Illinois to South Carolina by myself. I planned my departure date, checked the weather, oops, put it off. Planned another departure date, stressed that I couldn't get everything accomplished before my three-month trip, I put it off again. After calling my sister for a much-needed pep talk and boost of courage, I set the final date for my departure. I had marked out what I had thought was the halfway mark.

The first day of travel on straight, flat Illinois and Kentucky interstates proved to be a joyous time of worship music and taped sermons ending with a bit of political news. What a day! Exhausted but very proud of myself, I checked into my hotel and crashed for the night. Unfortunately, the caffeinated Coke I drank with my fast food supper interrupted my sleep; and at 2:30 a.m., I was awake and restless. I prayed, tossed and turned, listened to music, read, and watched television only to find myself still awake at 6:00 a.m. and panicking about the second half of the trip. I went back to sleep for an hour only to awake with memories of a bone-chilling nightmare about a creepy hotel! Debilitated by lack of sleep (of which I require a lot), I forced myself to eat breakfast, grabbed a couple of bananas for the road, and began to trudge on with the sound of worship music blaring so as to conjure a positive attitude for the journey ahead. Just as I had programmed my Garmin, I realized the depressing fact that I would lose an hour going east so the arrival time, instead of 5:00 pm, was now 6:00 p.m. This, since I can't drive well at night, also meant a race to be home before dark. Whew, I made it through Knoxville; and with the occasional uplifting phone calls from friends and family, I plugged along. I mean I REALLY plugged along.

Once again, I had forgotten an important obstacle in my drive home—mountains! I love riding through the mountains, but I came to realize I was scared of driving alone through the mountains. So I got in the truck lane and trudged along. I did not care that the trucks were passing me; my car was still moving. I looked at my Garmin and saw something I had not previously noticed. One of the boys had changed my little car on the road on my Garmin screen to a big bird flying. "But those who hope in the Lord will renew their strength. They will soar on wings like eagles, they will run and not grow weary, they will walk and not be faint" (Isa. 40:31). At that instant, I knew I would make it home. I practiced the presence of God on the road, through the mountains, with much fear, very tired, making it home right at dusk, all because I put my weight on the One who is always willing and able to hold me. No matter what. No matter where. No matter when.

IT'S ALL YOU. It's all on you, God.

Just Yesterday, I Could Hold You

In dictionary.com, the word "time," when used as a noun, has twenty-six definitions! As we've moved around, I have found just as many connotations to that same word. Since I am Southern by birth, I learned Southern time. Time to do an activity is described very clearly in one of three ways. A person is "ready," "right ready," or is "fixin' to be ready" to do something or go somewhere. We clearly understood the time element when using these words. When we moved to the country of Turkey, where drinking chi and socializing were paramount to business encounters, time was loosely based on the theme "when we get around to it." Our move to Guam taught us island time. Just don't worry about time at all. And in stark contrast, our next move to the Air Force Academy got us all straightened out and in line with the emphasis of military time—yes, the opposite of island time! Southern time, Turkey time, island time, military time, and to add a few more, this mom has to include husband time and child time, teenager time. Yes, the list is as exhaustive as is the definition, but overarching all our understanding of time is God's time.

We define time based on our cultural agenda. We say time is precious, time is money, time is valuable, time is manageable, time is measured, or time is wasted. We desire to hurry time or languish through time, but God, in His word, defines time in his infinite knowledge. He speaks of appointed time, proper time, created time, and eternity. In our lives, we have created a love-hate relationship with time. We read the part of scripture that says, "Outwardly we are wasting away" (2 Cor. 4:16), and sarcastically think, "Thanks for the truth of the Bible." Especially as we moms look in the mirror after a long day of wrangling with children. Or I look down at the sunspots on my arms and declare that I earned them time and again in the hot sun at baseball games. But the deeper truth is that time does change us: our shape, our age, our appearance, our abilities, our desires, and many other elements of our person.

Paradoxically as parents, we are inconsistent with our view of time—one minute, we can't wait for our children to be able to move to the next stage while at the same time desperately trying to hold on to the current stage. When they were little, I loved having the sweet little chubby baby feet to kiss on; but with time, they grew into big stinky, hairy hobbit feet that I wouldn't even want to touch. Holding my babies and picking them up to comfort was such a natural and important part of my life until one day, as time crept up, and I hauled my three-year-old Matt up in my arms to give that needed comfort. His legs were flailing about my knees, and my strength to hold the both of our weights was questionable. Time had changed me and Matt, and my back suggested that I just crouch down to give comfort from now on.

My word, I was wasting away! Some days, I mourned the accelerated passing of time; and other days, I prayed for the next stage to get here quickly! My firstborn seemed to have a personality defect every even year. It began, you guessed it, with the terrible twos. I struggled through that year by holding him tightly until he fell asleep after an exhausting bout of near-demon possessive rants throughout the house. I longed for the day when he turned three. For some reason, there were great seasons of calm for Ben between the even years, but I realized I couldn't skip whole years of enjoying my son's life wishing through to a better moment just because of a few temperament issues. Truthfully, Ben was a phenomenal joy despite the even-year troubles. Consequently, this narrative about Ben does illustrate a truth about our dilemma with time. As parents, we are eager for our children to talk, to walk, to play, to get friends, to play ball, to go to school, to go on their first date. The list goes on, and our life and family's life are marked by nothing more than looking forward to times and events. Things to look forward to and pictures to look backward on begin to mark our existence. Then panic sets in as time flies, and Ben, at his eighth-grade graduation announces, "You better enjoy me now. I will only be with you four more years." Is he serious? How could Ben put that pressure on me? How can I hold precious each moment of time with the strain to enjoy to the fullest?

I started writing this chapter when Ben was sixteen years old. He is now graduated from college, married, and expecting a baby. Now—I'm not finished yet—the baby is eight months old. For heaven's sake, I want to ask the question: where has the time gone, and why can't I hold on to it? I love family trips, fun times together, laughing, memories, Christmases, ballgames we all remember, family game nights, trips loaded in the van or trucks. But every one of those events comes and goes—makes me happy and then leaves me sad! Here lies the predicament. There are some parts of time I want to hold on to and guard without moving, and there are parts of time I want to get over quickly. We live by time. One night before bed, when Matt was just a toddler, he summed up how we live most of our life. "The clock says it's time for me to read my Bible" So we read! The clock says... Time. We love it, we hate it, we use it, we misuse it, we measure it, and we savor it. Although we did not create time nor do we control time, we know the One who does and is yet not bound by it.

The dilemma we face as parents is how to successfully enjoy the moment, savor the time, and live right now in God's appointed time, His proper time. Genesis 1 describes that in the beginning, God created time, day and night, and it was good. God created time for our benefit. God is eternal and doesn't need the measure of time. Ecclesiastes 3 reminds us that in parameters of time that God created, there is a specific time for each activity: "A time to be born and a time to die, a time to plant and a time to uproot, a time to kill and a time to heal, a time to tear down and a time to build, a time to weep and a time to laugh a time to mourn and a time to dance, a time to scatter stones and a time to gather them, a time to embrace and a time to refrain, a time to search and a time to give up, a time to keep and a time to throw away, a time to reap and a time to mend, a time to be silent and a time to speak, a time to love and a time to hate, a time for war and a time for peace."

But with that encyclopedic list of things to do with time comes the reminder that God has made everything beautiful in its time (Eccles. 3:11). For me, this scripture was practically manifested—a time to hold the baby and a time to let the baby cry in the crib, a time to do the dishes and a time to go play with the boys, a time to correct harshly and a time to show mercy, a time to question incessantly and a time to be quiet and observe, a time to teach and a time to learn, a time to sing and laugh with abandon and a time to hurt and cry, a time to fight for causes with the boys and a time to encourage the boys to fight alone, a time to hold on and a time to let go. But with the struggle of changing times, I must remember that He makes ALL things beautiful in His time.

God, in his wisdom, placed eternity in the hearts of men, yet we cannot fathom what God has done from beginning to end (Eccles. 3:11). Since we were created with that longing that only eternity will fill, we will continue to struggle with the good and bad constraints of time. But God is in control; therefore, we do not waste time for God uses all things for His purpose. Our duty is to consider the words of Mordecai to Esther, "who knows but that you have come to this royal position for such a time as this" (Esther 4:14b).

Car trips proved to be times of valuable conversation, so I always listened as the boys would discuss the sweetest subjects. On the way to Liberty Farms in Valdosta, Georgia, when the boys were preschoolers, Matt led with the precious declaration, "Mama, Jesus gave me and Ben to you."

Before I could respond, Ben added with great innocence, "I bet He wanted to keep me and Matt." Maybe so, I pondered, but this was my time to have a royal position—being mom to Ben and Matt. At God's perfect time, at His appointed time, He sent them to me.

"Get out of the way! Matt, stop right now!" I screeched while running as fast as I could behind my five-year-old maniac on a Big Wheel. The Turkish gardeners were jumping off the sidewalk, as if being parted by God like the Red Sea, for fear of getting struck by a mad cyclist yelling and laughing at the top of his lungs. After passing through several stop signs, which Matt flew through unfazed by the word on the sign, the possible traffic, or the crazed woman running behind him trying to stop him, the saga finally ended. My little hoodlum was caught, and I was exhausted! That is something that I did—could do—when Matt was four. Could I do that now? Would I do that now? You might say that I am outwardly wasting away, and that is the reason why I couldn't or wouldn't do that now. But you might also say as the conclusion of that verse states, "We are inwardly being renewed day by day" (2 Cor. 4:16b). Time is an educator. Time is good to me, and it has taught me many lessons. For one: don't chase the four-year-old on a Big Wheel because it only makes him want to play and go faster.

Time has given me wisdom. Day by day, through all our times, God has enhanced my understanding that He created time for us. Everything has a season for us to enjoy. Often in scripture, Jesus said, "My time has not yet come." On this earth, Jesus was constrained by time as we are, but not one minute of his time was wasted. Psalm 90:12 says, "Teach us to number our days that we might gain a heart of wisdom." With all the wisdom I can muster, I have learned to stop struggling so much against time and can honestly say that I loved the times with my small boys. I loved the times with my medium-sized boys, I love the times with my large boys, and I will forever love the times with the men my boys have become. Now I will love the time with my daughter-in-law, my grandson, and in the right time, another daughter-in-law and grandsons. Maybe even granddaughters. With wisdom comes the eternal acknowledgement that "my times are in your hands" (Ps. 31:15a).

Are We There Yet?

Every family has probably experienced the familiar vacation question being yelled from the back of the minivan, "Are we there yet?" To a child, a mile on the road seems like endless minutes that become hours and days and eternity. And their minds can't fathom that asking the same question a million times will not make us get to our destination any faster. Ben was the most impatient with our trips, so after banning his questions, he began singing with made-up tunes. "How many more mile-ees? How many more mile-ees? I'm tired as an elephant," and the song would go on. I must say I enjoyed the advances in technology when we could get a small television with built-in VCR, but even more as we truly progressed to a van with a DVD player.

The boys were leaving home one by one, going to college, becoming young men, and I was left with an empty house and an empty heart. For the last eighteen to twenty years, my life as a stay-at-home mom had revolved around them! My job had been to make sure they grew physically, socially, spiritually, emotionally, and were prepared for this day, the day they would leave the house. Now I sat in my silent disbelief and wondered, *Is my job over? Have I just been fired? Are we really there yet?*

Yes, I had even exhibited signs of panic. The word "panic" is defined as a sudden, overwhelming fear, with or without cause, that produces hysterical or irrational behavior. On one of my worst days, I began gardening—something I never enjoyed doing! The summer was over, and both boys had gone to college. I was working outside, first in the small unattended flower garden. Then I had plans to groom the dog (seemed desperate for things to fill my day) and whatever other outside chores I could find to look busy. I had left the door open and heard the phone ring. It was Ben from his college in South Carolina. He gave a short update about his adventures, and I listened. No need to ask questions or respond, he had an agenda and a specific time limit. As I headed back to my weeds, I mean, garden, I mulled over that great little interruption. Ben just needed to touch base to give a report and to perhaps get some validation. Two or three weeds later, several texts came in on my cell phone. So with much messier hands, I responded to a frantic Matt who had some life-altering need that required my immediate attention—probably gas money.

A sense of relief overshadowed my panic that day. The same interruptions of my chores that I experienced when the boys were three and five or ten and twelve were now occurring at nineteen and twenty-one. And they weren't even at home! I did a happy dance in my heart that day as I answered my own questions. I will always have a job. I will always be Mom. We were not there yet.

On break from college, my youngest son, Matt, seemed perplexed with a dilemma that had plagued his thoughts. Growing up, Matt always would say to me, "You are my favorite lady in the whole world." Anxiously and without wanting to hurt anyone's feelings, Matt now questioned how he would express that feeling toward me when he got married. Choosing to answer his concern with as much thoughtfulness as it was asked, I just explained that he could say to me, "You are my favorite mama in the whole world." When his wife had children, he could say to me, "You are my favorite grandmamma in the whole world." Things can change, but we aren't there yet.

Looking back now, I realize that things were always changing incrementally. God used Beanie Babies to show me that change is real and that I have to adjust. While living in Turkey, the boys began collecting Beanie Babies. There was only one store on base, so it was quite a treat when new stocks arrived, and we ran to select the perfect one. As the tradition began each Christmas, I enthusiastically and carefully selected the perfect Beanie Baby for each boy's stocking. When the stockings were attacked on Christmas morning, the satisfaction of my selection was rewarded with hugs and excitement until one December, Ben sheepishly approached me and suggested that he may not want a Beanie Baby in his stocking this year. Are you kidding? What happened? Don't you love Beanie Babies? It had to be said. "Mom, I think I have outgrown Beanie Babies!" With that revelation, I knew things would just keep changing.

It happened again one morning at breakfast. Every morning, I delighted in—maybe "delighted in" is too strong—well, I fixed the boys breakfast. They especially seemed to enjoy grits, eggs over easy, and bacon all smashed together. Because I knew they enjoyed this breakfast, I made it over and over and over again. One morning, Matt was chosen as spokesperson, as always, and timidly suggested that maybe they could just have cereal or pop tarts for a while. Upon further investigation, I learned that they had wanted a different breakfast for a long time, but were afraid to speak up because they knew I enjoyed fixing it for them. They chose to be stuck in a breakfast pattern because they didn't want to hurt my feelings. My sweet boys helped me grow that day as a mom. I can't be static in a pattern or role of mothering just because it is comfortable to me. I realized that as they grew, my role would need to decrease as their independence increased.

This would happen many more times as the boys grew. My selections, opinions, and control in their decisions would decrease as they matured and discovered their own likes and dislikes, and began to assert their own control over their lives. As I saw it, my options for response were slim. I could continue to press on as usual with the role that I wanted to play in their life, or I could let change happen and let them grow. In the process, I discovered that being a mom means that I will grow just as much as my children.

God was gracious with the baby steps of my changing roles throughout the years. Early on, I picked out clothes for them and dressed them, then they gradually dressed themselves in the clothes I had purchased. Eventually, they wanted to pick out clothes with my assistance, but now they just want the cash. Early on, I taught them their ABCs and 123s, eventually assisting them with homework and tests others had taught them, but now I encourage and pray and pray and pray and pray as they control their learning. Early on, I was solely in charge of their food. I nursed them, then spoon fed them, then put the food on the plate for them to eat, but eventually, they ate without help and chose what they wanted. Now, I just send food, care packages, charge their meal card at school, fill them up when they come home, and hope for the best. One day, our checkbook will rejoice when they are completely in charge of this area. Early on, I chauffeured them everywhere they went. Gradually, they were driving with us in the car, and then they were driving alone (again with much prayer). And now when they are home, they drive me around. Early on, I chose the hairstyles for the boys and told the barber what to do. As time passed, they made choices about their hair, and they asked me to cut it like they wanted. But now, whether it is a buzz cut or Mohawk or long and straggly bed head, I just encourage—not really—I tell the honest truth!

Letting go, progressing through the changes of being mom as they need and giving up my control is hard! There is one mom from the Old Testament that I am reminded of who gave over control of her child. Hannah, whose story is recorded in the Old Testament, wanted a child so badly but was barren for years. She wept and fervently prayed for a child, pledging that if God gave her a child, she would give him back to the Lord for all the days of his life (1 Sam. 1:11). The Bible records, "In the course of time, Hannah gave birth to a son and called him Samuel" (1 Sam. 1:20). As the story goes, Hannah stayed with Samuel, raised and nurtured him until the time was right for him to be weaned; and at that time, she took him to Eli and offered him to live there with the priest as giving him to the Lord. As Hannah gave Samuel to Eli, she said, "So now I give him to the Lord, his whole life will be given to the Lord" (1 Sam. 1:28)

When the boys were babies, Greg and I came before the church; and in a symbolic act, we gave them to the Lord. We presented them to God. By dedicating them to the Lord, we stated that they would be raised in a home that serves and honors God. We stated that we as their parents would teach them about the love of God and His word. Every night as I tucked the boys in, I prayed that they would "grow in wisdom and stature and favor with God and man" (1 Sam. 2:26, Luke 2:52).

Now the boys have grown and left home for college. Letting go and allowing them to grow and make mistakes is tough! I'm sure it was also hard for Hannah to take her weaned child and allow him to finish growing at the house of the priest. But she had done her part as she fed him and taught him until he was weaned. While in my house, I fed the boys all kinds of ways and taught them. Now they are weaned—no longer totally dependent on me for their growth. I have done my part physically just as Hannah, and now I have to hand over control. Even more, I find myself giving them over to God. Pleading with Him to help them grow, help them make good choices, help them flee temptation, and mostly help them grow more in their relationship with God.

I love the rest of the story of Hannah. First Samuel 2:19 informs us that each year, Hannah made her son a little robe and took it to him when she went with her husband to offer the annual sacrifice. She was not there yet! Hannah was always Samuel's mom; the roles were just different now. Whew, what a relief to this newly empty nester!

Sometimes in my neighborhood, I see moms with their toddlers doing "mom things," and my heart aches a moment. Sometimes, Greg and I take off to Branson or other "exotic locations" just because we are not tied down with endless ballgames, and that's fun! Sometimes, I see pictures of my boys when they are young and have a longing in my heart for those days. Sometimes, when Greg and I want to go out to eat on a Tuesday night and not cook, we just go for it! These schizophrenic feelings are a part of my role now as an empty nester. I realize this is not good or bad, just part of my process. Sometimes I have to grieve the roles that I no longer have and sometimes I have to celebrate the roles that I have now! It is freeing to accept the changes, embrace the changes, and not to fear that I will ever, "Be there yet."

If you think about it, God never finishes parenting us. We grow and we change, and our needs are different. But there is never a time when we don't need our Heavenly Father. We are never there yet. Greg teases me about my calling my daddy to ask him questions that Greg has already answered, but Greg knows that my daddy will forever have a role in my life, and I will forever be his Kathy Doodle.

My boys, who are now 6'2" and over 6'5", may be much taller than I am, but I am still their mama. Randomly, my phone may beep with an incoming text with my favorite message, "I love you, mama!" With those important words, and especially the word "mama," I am encouraged that I am still Mom and that we are "not there yet."

So what's my role now? Well, I can just tell you about today because tomorrow, it may change. I don't have physical control of their growth, but I still have a part. The struggle for me has been to discern what my role is now. I always question myself, "Do I call? Do I text? Do I ask endless questions? Do I give advice, or do I just watch?" As I continue to wrestle with these conundrums, I have decided on two courses of action. I will always encourage their growth in the Lord, and I will always pray. This may not be the physical work I used to have, but it is the hard work. Hannah's son, Samuel, grew up listening to the Lord, and ministering to the Lord. He became a prophet in Israel. So I hear his words to Israel as my continued role as Mama: "As for me, far be it from me that I should sin against the Lord by failing to pray for you. And I will teach you the way that is good and right. But be sure to fear the Lord and serve him faithfully with all your heart; consider what great things he has done for you" (1 Sam. 12:23)

No, we are not there yet. I'm a grandmamma now!

What Grade Did I Make?

I absolutely loved school! I know that sounds crazy to many of you. I do like to learn, but I don't think I loved it just because learning was fun. I liked the grades! Now the reason I liked the grades was because I got good ones. The feeling of having a paper handed back with a big red 100% on it was invigorating! Okay, call me a nerd, but I enjoyed being rewarded for the effort I had put into the work. I enjoyed getting a grade for what I did. Early in life, I appreciated that I could receive validation just by making good grades. So from kindergarten to elementary school to middle school, high school, college, and graduate school, I acquired much positive validation as I went straight through from one school to the next. Receiving validation was certainly not the reason for going to school, but the accolades provided great encouragement for me to do my best. I did good work; I got a good grade.

I finally stopped going to school, and I got a job. It was a day of rejoicing for my parents who had believed that I would just attend school for the rest of my life. My first job out of Seminary was a hospice social worker. You would think in the work of death and dying, there were few rewards, but it was just the opposite. Although the work was tough many days, our hospice director had enacted a method whereby family members of patients with whom we had worked could send us messages as encouragement. Just one such note supporting and affirming my ministry to these patients and their families encouraged me to continue the work. When Greg finished Seminary, we moved to South Carolina where he began a civilian pastorate, and I began a job as clinical supervisor for the Alcohol and Drug Commission. With much less means of validation in this job, I began a "kudos" envelope—for my eyes only. This envelope contained positive comments from others or good things happening with clients I had helped. My kudos envelope contained any note of encouragement that I could look at on days where I wondered if what I was doing had produced any lasting results.

I know I am not the only one who likes to get kudos! Be truthful. Do you like getting credit for what you do, a pat on the back, or just good strokes? As Christians, we may be appalled at the thought that we would desire or need this validation or kudos. And to be honest, I never really gave it a thought until the day came when these tangible methods of affirmation were gone. No more grades, no more raises at work, no more comments from patients or clients that I had helped, no more "kudos envelopes." Those tangible affirmations or validations vanished the day I chose to become a stay-at-home mom, or so I thought.

Greg went to work every day and received encouraging words from those he counseled, doting affirmations about his sermon that had blessed his parishioners, stellar comments from his boss about the program for airmen he directed that reached hundreds, and promotion boards that directly validated his good work. You are probably thinking, "Wow, that woman is bitter. She has issues!" No, I love my husband and am so proud of his phenomenal accolades, but I have to admit, in my daily work that took place in tattered clothes as not to worry when spit upon, endless loads of cloths to wash, and things to pick up, mouths to feed, books to read, fights to break up—you know, the list—I began to look at me and my need for validation. I have to admit, as a stay-at-home mom, I struggled to know and to feel that my contribution was worth the work that I was doing. Some days it didn't seem like it. Then I had to ask myself, "What did I want?" What type of validation did I need? What was enough for me?

Several verses began to flood my mind to remind me that God's affirmation is enough for me. Psalm 73:26 says, "My flesh and my heart may fail, but God is the strength of my heart and my portion forever." Psalm 119:57 relates my desire, "You are my portion, O Lord, I have promised to obey your words." Lamentations 3:24 states, "I say to myself the Lord is my portion, therefore I will wait for him." God is my portion. God is all that I need. Who needs earthly affirmations? Yet I longed for a tangible expression. As one of my boys said one night when afraid and I boldly announced they need not be afraid because Jesus was with them, "That's great, Mama, but I would like Jesus with skin." They desired to see physically. And in my childlike state, I desired also to have physical endorsement of my work as a mom.

Since I enjoyed school so much, I set out to explore and to learn the answers to the questions and struggles that I was now facing as a stay-at-home mom. I will assure you that it was a process of growing into my new role and my new understanding of validation. As I looked back on things, I was being validated from the first day my first baby was born. When the baby was hungry and cried, the nurse brought the baby to me to feed. I was the only one able to give the baby what he needed. The validation began as it was determined that I alone, at that moment, was responsible for the growth and nourishment of this miniature human being. From countless hugs and kisses with dirty little hands, to creative artwork proudly displayed on the refrigerator, to the thousand times I heard from precious lips the word "mama," I began to log affirmations.

Soon the biggest of rewards would come, and I once again would be amazed that God so beautifully affirmed my parenthood. My purpose was great, even greater than I had first imagined! Only a few months after Ben's second birthday, I overheard him, while pointing to a statue of Jesus in the chapel, tell Greg's boss, "That was the Lord and God." The seed that was planted on a daily basis by a mom in pajamas and unkempt hair had taken root. The seed grew, and God allowed me to see that growth in Ben. Two months before his fourth birthday, Ben explained to me, "Mama, if I asked Jesus in my heart, He will be my Savior." Even though he also made me aware that he had heard this from Psalty the Singing Songbook, whom he dearly loved, it was validation enough for the one who put in the VHS tape! The seed that was knowledge began to grow more deeply when in April, before Ben's fifth birthday, he asked me a very important question, "Mama, am I a Christian?" I eagerly explained what it meant to personally recognize our need for Jesus as our Savior, ask for forgiveness, and invite Him into our life. He listened and responded, "I want to be one, but not right now. I want to pray first, or I will get shy and begin to cut up." Ben prayed, I prayed, Greg prayed, we all prayed! In March of 1998, for days, Ben came to me or to Greg revealing things he had done in the past that were burdening him. What could possibly burden a five-year-old? Sin! He confessed his guilt over throwing out peas he told me that he had eaten. He confessed that he blamed Matt for something that he had done. Ben finally announced that he was a bad person. The seed of knowledge had grown to become the conviction of the Holy Spirit. That day, Ben confessed his sin and professed Christ as his Lord and his Savior. Ben completed his day with a prayer, "Jesus, thank you for reminding me that I need you." I also completed my day with a prayer, "Jesus, thank you for this eternal validation of being a mother, a son's salvation."

After that night, Ben's burden changed. He no longer had the weight of his sin, but he carried weight of desire that his little brother Matt would know Jesus. Ben asked me over and over again, even to the point of tears at times, to teach Matt about Jesus also. Although we taught Matt just as we had Ben, he began his own campaign of teaching. He told Matt about Jesus's name and told Matt that Jesus is God. Matt had seen that Ben invited Jesus in his life. The seed was planted, but it had to grow. Matt was angry and pouted every time Ben was able to participate in the Lord's Supper. Each time, he would declare that he wanted to ask Jesus to come into his life. Life was never "fair" in Matt's mind, and he had a hard time taking personal responsibility; so we prayed that his knowledge would grow into understanding. Something began to change in Matt's heart. As "unfairness" turned to conviction. Many, many days, Matt got off the bus from kindergarten and quickly blurted out things that he had done wrong during the school day. He had never gotten in trouble for any of the events he had mentioned. In fact, he said he didn't think anyone even knew that he had called someone a bad word under his breath or that he had stuck out his tongue at someone. But he had told the boy he was sorry anyway, and now he was asking about the punishment he should receive. He wanted to know if Jesus was mad at him. I explained that Jesus did not like what he did, but that if he asked Jesus to forgive him, Jesus would forget it. "But," Matt said, "if I don't ask forgiveness, Jesus can't forget it." After several months of daily conviction and of being scared to sleep, Matt finally told me that Jesus was knocking at the door of his heart. In June of 2000, Matt opened his heart's door, accepted Christ's forgiveness, and became a Christian. The reason Matt gave to me that night was, "Because I love Him." I love Jesus too! He loves me enough to give authentication of my momhood, one son being instrumental in the salvation of the other!

We were thrilled about Matt's decision for Christ, but quite apprehensive when his first grade teacher called to discuss his vocal faith. Thankfully, our uneasiness was short lived as we heard the teacher's commentary. Matt had been telling the students that Jesus was the only way to get to heaven. A discussion erupted, and Matt brought another child up to the teacher so she could validate his conviction. Matt's teacher wanted us to explain to Matt that while she could not confirm his convictions to the other students in the classroom, she certainly agreed with his convictions and encouraged Matt to continue his evangelistic efforts. So he did! In fifth grade, he brought his best friend to Jesus stating, "Mama, I want my friend in heaven with me." Just the other morning—3:45 a.m. to be exact—I received a text message from Matt from college. "Great news! My roommate just prayed to receive Christ!'"

Proverbs 31 says, "Her children will rise up and call *her* blessed," but I have learned that the kudos are from your children rising up and being a blessing to others. His senior year in high school, Ben was in a relationship that at the beginning seemed innocent and truthful, but we discovered later that it was all a lie and deception. In the midst of deep hurt and embarrassment, the first word out of my seventeen-year-old son's mouth was "I forgive her. I am a Christian. That is all I can do!"

Here's what I learned from my research. No one cares what grades you made in school. The nice words that people say only last for a short time. The money you make from a job well done gets spent.

Singing during the worship service one Sunday, I stopped and strained to hear a slightly monotone sound next to me. As the sound got more audible, I heard the words, "Make me more like you, Lord" coming from my fourteen-year-old son. I quit singing and just listened. As I began to cry, heart pounding almost out of my chest, I thanked God for His validation. My days in "mama clothes" and endless trips from place to place and sacrifices of my time that I thought were wasted were at that moment given a stamp of well done—your work is purposeful. I thought to myself, *Sing louder, son. Sing louder.* I learned that my greatest validation, accolade, kudos was not something that would last only for a moment, but something of eternal value—a Christian child that loves Jesus and carries on the faith so that others will know.

Luke 1:14 is now in my Kudos envelope: "He will be a joy and delight to you, and many will rejoice because of his birth."

He Never Quits!

We might be the first Southern Baptist chaplain and family excommunicated from our church because their son finally began utilizing lessons taught for years. Eighth grade was a trying, somewhat-difficult year academically for Matt, and for Greg and me. He made good grades, but they came with a struggle. It seemed that writing your name on your paper was a skill that Matt had failed to pick up in the first grade, so we had to literally prod him on a daily basis to put his name on his schoolwork. Matt even enlisted the help of his older, wiser brother who had mastered the skill many years ago. Ben's compelling yet simple advice seemed to be the catalyst for Matt. "I always write my name on the paper first." As Matt's adherence to this new skill grew, so did our glee over his accomplishment.

One particular Sunday, our glee turned to "oops." Let me say up front that Greg and I had spoken openly and in front of the boys about some negative things that were happening in our church. It turned out that maybe we shared too openly and without some discretionary instructions. That Sunday during dinner, Matt proudly announced that he had participated in a survey about the church that was given in his Sunday school class that morning. He reported that he had been brutally honest about the areas he felt were wrong or lacking in the church. And then beaming with accomplishment and pride, Matt announced to the family that before he answered a single question, he wrote his name on the paper!

Matt had learned and applied the lesson we had taught; but obviously, we still had more teaching, and he had more learning to accomplish. Parenting does not end with each new lesson learned; it just changes and broadens. It is a continual process. We still work at helping our children grow, learn, and become productive and godly adults. Sometimes, the process is frustrating, but we don't quit. We don't stop parenting because our children didn't get it the first time, or because they stumbled but they grew some, or because they were not learning as fast as we desired. We keep on working because we are their parents, and they are our children. Sounds much like another parent that we sing about:

> "He's still working on me, to make me what I
> ought to be. It took Him just a week to make the
> moon and stars, the sun, and the earth and Jupiter
> and Mars. How loving and patient He must be,
> 'cause He's still working on me!" (Joel Hemphill).

Work is defined as the exertion of effort directed to produce or accomplish something. Workmanship is defined as the product or result of labor and skill or work executed. "For we are God's workmanship created in Christ Jesus to do good works which God prepared in advance for us to do" (Eph. 2:10) Greg began taking the boys to the baseball field to play when they were very small. Matt would see Ben hit the ball, run the bases, and squeal as Dad ran after him, then catching him and scooping him up to belly zerberts and great laughter. Matt, even as early as two years old, grabbed a bat and tried to emulate the antics of his older brother. He hit the ball and began to run the bases, squealing as Dad ran behind him trying to catch him. He made it to first base, then second base, and then skipping third, Matt ran over the pitcher's mound directly to home plate where Dad scooped him up amid wild laughter. Matt didn't follow the rules of baseball at that time. There was no umpire present to call him out for skipping third base. He had to learn. There was work to be done with Matt's baseball knowledge.

We were having missionaries come to speak at our church, and I was explaining to our four-year-old Ben how interesting the slides of the missionaries would be. He seemed very excited all Sunday afternoon about the prospects of the missionary slides at church that night, and I was truly taken aback and thrilled at his interest. During the entire service, Ben listened intently but kept looking at me as if something were wrong. After the service, he disappointedly turned to me and innocently challenged, "Mom, where is the missionary's slide?" You see, the only slide my son knew about was the one in our backyard or on the playground. All afternoon, he was excited about the prospects of a jungle gym being erected in the sanctuary. His use of the English language had to grow. He had to learn. There was work to be done in teaching Ben the different meanings of words.

There were so many things as babies, then toddlers, then adolescents, and then young men that the boys would have to learn. Ben had to learn that you didn't take off all the angels from the Christmas tree just because you were pretending to shoot all the birds. Matt had to learn that when his dad said, "Pinch your cheeks," in order wait to find a bathroom on a trip, he didn't mean hold your face cheeks until they turned red. I also had to learn as the boys were growing. I learned to frisk them before church. Yes, the preacher's wife was looking for contraband in the form of Game Boys. The contraband later morphed into pocketknives, hunting knives, any kind of knives. Our last attempt to a visit a National Park with Ben resulted in turning back to the car to get rid of the knife in his sock. I had to learn many ways to reduce odor in a car, in shoes, in football pads, and in every room of the house. As I parented, my knowledge grew, and through good and bad circumstances, I persisted in my work to raise the boys. The Bible explains the phenomena in terms of first drinking milk then going to solid food.(Heb. 5:12, 14). We first have elementary knowledge and then we grow.

But how can I love a child so very, very much yet be so angry and frustrated at him? I guess I stopped asking the question when one day, God whispered to me during an adult meltdown, "Kathy, I have the same thought about you." What I am about to say sounds like I might be a Baptist preacher. I guess being married to one for over thirty years counts too. But that little song about God still working on me brings three points to mind: in our parenting, we have to be patient, loving, and just keep working. At the same time we are parenting our children, God is parenting us. Jesus said to them, "My Father is always at his work to this very day, and I too am working" (John 5:17).

God is working; as He works, his character is revealed in His work. "But you, O Lord, are a compassionate and gracious God, slow to anger, abounding in love and faithfulness" (Ps. 86:15). Oops, our character is also revealed in our work. The attributes that I lacked sometimes in my parenting that God has in abundance are persistence and patience. In the midst of frustration at the boys' behavior, let down over their lack of growth in a particular area, annoyance over general disobedience, or irritation with not understanding their needs at a particular stage, I kept working, kept parenting; but oftentimes with a lack of composure, calmness, and perseverance that enabled me to consistently parent with confidence and resoluteness. At those moments, I had to look to the One parenting me. Colossians 4:17 gave me the encouragement to always "see to it that you complete the work that you have received in the Lord."

As a mom, you can't quit! Psalm 138:8 reassures me constantly that the Lord will fulfill His purpose for me and my children, His love endures forever, and He will not abandon the work of His hands. I won't either. I never wanted to quit parenting the boys. I love them with all my heart. But sometimes, I wanted to hide. Sometimes, I wanted time alone. Sometimes, I wanted to take a long break. It seemed that Matt would never learn to get his homework out of his locker and turn it in, but he did (we got rid of the locker). Because Ben had such a hard time initiating conversation with people, I wondered how in the world he would grow in this skill, but he learned. He is now a respected Army officer leading his men. I felt so often that we would go over the same lessons with the boys over and over and over again, but they eventually got it. "Therefore since through God's mercy we have this ministry, we do not lose heart" (2 Cor. 4:1). God will fulfill His purpose with our parenting and in our children's lives (Ps. 57:2). He doesn't quit. He doesn't give up. He will finish the work.

When the boys were very young, we rode with them on the merry-go-round. Since this was one of Greg's favorite activities, he usually rode and I took pictures. As they grew, the boys rode alone, and we both waved and took pictures from the sidelines. Even when the boys didn't see us around the backside of the merry-go-round, they knew we were there. Whether we were visible beside them or watching from the side, we didn't abandon our job of being present. Even when we don't see God working, we can trust His heart. We trust that He has a plan for our children: "'For I know the plans I have for you,' declares the Lord, 'plans to prosper you and not to harm you, plans to give you hope and a future'" (Jer. 29:11).

The boys are older now, and Ben even has a son of his own. Our work as parents is more on watching from the sidelines and offering encouragement and prayer. One summer, we had a yard sale. The boys were trying to earn some extra money to take to college. Ben found a box with a model A-10 airplane that he and Greg began putting together when he was just a boy. I asked if he just wanted to throw it out. "No," Ben replied, "Dad and I will finish it one day. We will finish what we started."

In my Bible, I carry a picture of Ben hitting a baseball off a tee at one of his early t-ball games. I have a picture of Matt with a Carolina Panthers football uniform on when he was just two. Why do I carry these crazy pictures in my Bible? It's proof! God worked in the lives of these two little boys and has now made them men. I don't know how He did it, but He did. And He allowed me to be a part of the work. Because of His promise, He will keep on working in the lives of my boys, and their wives and their children. "Being confident of this, that he who began a good work in you will carry it on to completion until the day of Christ Jesus" (Phil. 1:6). "God, who has called you into fellowship with his Son Jesus Christ our Lord, is faithful" (1 Cor. 1:9). God works! He never quits!

Home

"Leave your country, your people and your father's household, and go to the land I will show you" (Gen. 12:1). Do this every two or three years. We are not Abraham, but we are a military family. Separating life into piles is the first step: piles going to Goodwill, piles to be thrown out, piles for storage, piles for the moving truck, and piles to hand carry. The next steps include collecting medical records for each family member from doctors all over town, planning the shutoff of services, arranging address changes, and saying a proper good bye to friends you grew to love in a short amount of time. All this leads up to the day when the smell of hundreds of boxes and the sound of pulling tape and the rattling of paper envelopes your house, as strangers invade your home and haul out your life and move it to the next house. "See I am sending an angel ahead of you to guard you along the way, to bring you to the place I have prepared" (Exod. 23:20).

The research about our new duty station has been done, and everyone is excited about the prospects of the next place we will live: a new place to put our stuff, to make new friends, to start new ministry, to create new memories with a new address and a new house that we will make a home—at least temporarily. Home is a simple word, yet it is laden with different meanings that stir up various emotions. A shelter where people reside is the most basic of definitions. We have lived in a 1950s unrenovated base house with parquet floors and tiny closets. We lived in a small 900-square foot shelter in a foreign land that had one bathroom and two bedrooms. We lived in a stucco block structure with amazing outdoor amenities. We lived in a concrete bunker that could withstand 250 mph typhoon winds. We lived in rentals and in shelters that we had purchased, but all of them just started out as houses, as shelters.

But then we put our stuff in the shelter, we live our life in the shelter, and the roof over our head was transformed by definition from house to home—a place where domestic affections are centered. The same pictures were hung in Turkey as were hung in Georgia. The same furniture was placed in the family room in Guam as was in the expansive house in Albuquerque. Each piece was deliberately placed to create our home out of a house. Although not quite as deliberately as Ben had thought. Day after day, moms are able to catch and know what children are doing. Children come to believe that moms have eyes in the back of their head or some special powers. But not Ben. He had figured it all out, and I overheard him educating his younger brother Matt on how Mom knew so much about what they did. Ben had surmised that I had placed pictures and mirrors all over the house at precise angles so that I could, through the glared image, spy on them wherever they were in the house. And I recreated the same effect at every house. I appreciate the credit that Ben was giving me for this enormous feat of meticulous engineering, but I was just placing pictures around a house to make a shelter a home.

A car passes us on the interstate, and we immediately feel a kinship with the driver because of the Palmetto Tree and a Half Moon sticker on their car. It's the flag of South Carolina. South Carolina is home, defined by as the place or region that is native or common. Just crossing the state line led to shouts of "whoop whoop" in the car, and a feeling of excitement and connectedness that came from being around the "familiar." To a military kid, this sense of belonging to a region or place is challenging. My youngest son had only lived in South Carolina for five months before we entered Active Duty Military service. One day, I greatly offended his sense of belonging when I jokingly questioned his determined loyalty to South Carolina when talking to his friends. "After all," I remarked, "you don't even remember living there. It was only for five months." He quickly and vehemently defended his position, "Mama, you raised me, and you are from South Carolina. That's where Papa lives and that's where I am from! I am a Southern boy!" Just like Matt, we knew in our hearts where home was, but what were we supposed to put on paper and tell people?

Ben first brought this dilemma to our attention when filling out forms for college, and he asked, "Mom, where am I from?" "Ben, do you mean what is your home of record? Or what is your current address? Or where do you CALL home?" He took off for college and quickly learned that kids really did not want to take the time to find out the answer to a simple question posed to a military kid: "Where are you from, Ben?" After the first few times Ben answered, "I was born in South Carolina, then moved to Georgia, Turkey, Albuquerque, Guam, and Colorado Springs; but my parents live in Clovis, New Mexico, but I am a technically a resident of Florida," the other college kids passed the word around. "Don't ask Woodbury where he is from unless you have a while to listen."

I have a pillow in my family room with the outline of the state of South Carolina with the word "home" inside the outline of the state. The writing on the pillow sums up the nature of our connectedness to this place: "The Palmetto State, Beautiful Beaches, where tea is sweet, accents are sweeter, pearls and flip flops are staples, biscuits and gravy are vegetables, long cotton farm fields, wide front porches, friendly folks, and people with good manners, the days are warm and faith is strong. Every conversation starts with y'all and ends with blessing hearts. It's a place that will get in your blood and call you back wherever you go." That's my home. They talk like me, think like me, value similar things that I do. They shop at the Piggly Wiggly. They know how I grew up. It's just a small region of the country—nothing fancy, for sure—but it's home.

No matter where we lived, we always looked forward to going back. It was the place I lived since I was in the fifth grade. It was a very modest, brick ranch home on about eight acres of land on the outskirts of a small farming community in South Carolina. My mom and dad created a haven for the family inside and outside of their home. We walked in the door and Mom greeted us with hugs and the smell of Southern food and of course, brownies. Dad had designed a playground of exploration with a four-stable horse barn and a bunkhouse with ping-pong table, pool table, Jacuzzi, and a refrigerator stocked with prizes for the grandchildren and big kids too. This was our place of refuge or retreat—which is the most essential and purposeful definition of home.

A place of shelter, protection, or safety is the definition of "refuge," and a place of seclusion and safety defines a "retreat." Both describe a home where children grow in security, in sanctuary, in freedom to be themselves. As parents, it is our responsibility to provide a place—a home—where our children are safe to be who they are, to grow, to make mistakes, to learn, to feel safe to question, to feel, and to want to come home to.

A call came from the school reporting that Matt was in the nurse's office complaining of feeling sick. We have always had stringent rules concerning going to school and being "sick"; therefore, a stomachache or various other created infirmities rarely made the cut for consideration to stay home. Blood, fever, or broken bones usually had to accompany the complaint for there to be a sick day. When I arrived at the school, Matt was moaning and wailing of massive pains in his stomach. So in front of an extremely sympathetic nurse, I chose to take Matt home with the strictest of instructions. He would go straight to bed and would not be allowed to play or watch television while we monitor his ailment. Quite miraculously, within a few minutes of arriving at home, Matt was healed! His pains were gone! Of course, my motherly interrogation began as I wondered what could possibly be going on at school that my third grader had to escape with a pretend stomachache. Was it a bully? Was it a test? Did he forget homework and get scared? Knowing Matt, none of these three options seemed radical enough to cause this behavior. Ultimately, he confessed. Before school, he was playing with his GI Joes, and he accidently had placed the green plastic one-inch GI Joe gun in his backpack. When he pulled out his homework, he spied the contraband, remembered the no-tolerance policy on weapons in school, and panicked. He placed the object in his pocket, but it was searing his conscience and he had to find safety before someone found him out. He had to think of a way out; he knew he had to get home! He needed his place of refuge!

This past year, we sold my mom and dad's house, and my parents moved to a more manageable living situation. The whole family gathered at the home place which had become our landing place and boxed up belongings, sifted through memories, found hidden treasures, separated keepsakes, and threw out or gave away the unwanted. My sister got the bookshelves, Dad's big desk, and various items from their house. I got the rocking chair where all of the grandbabies were soothed and the dining table where the family gathered for meals and long conversations. My niece, nephews, sons, and brother also got other sacred items that came from our family's place that was our harbor. The sentiment we attached to this piece of real estate was strong, and the memories of love and home were real. But as the couches left and the boxes packed up, we took the most prized possessions and the ones who created that haven of security with us. Our mom and dad were the real refuge. It was not the home but the ones who made the home.

As a baby and as a toddler, Matt held my hair and twisted it around his finger for comfort and a feeling of safety. Greg tried to lie down with him during an especially needy time one night, and Matt refused his offer explaining, "I need real hair." He needed Mama's hair, not short Daddy hair. I have a teddy bear that Greg gave me the Valentine's Day before we were married. That bear has been through many an airport carried by hand, until the boys got too old to carry Mama's teddy bear (then it was in the suitcase). That bear obviously has no special power, but it somehow brings a sense of comfort of security, of home. It was never the shelter, the place, nor a thing that made a home for our boys; it was always the family, the being together. Our motto as a military family was "Home is where the Air Force sends us." It didn't matter the location or the structure of our dwelling. It just mattered that we were together, and we built a home. As Greg and I moved from country to country, from state to state, from house to house, creating a place of security and refuge for our boys was our top priority. Moving every two or three years was sometimes challenging, but we always took our home with us: a place of refuge, a place where the boys would know peace, security, unconditional love, and acceptance.

My older sister and I usually got along famously growing up; but there were times when we argued, fought, or said things we shouldn't. "You're so sheltered!" was the remark blurted out to me one day. I absorbed this statement, in the connotation in which it was given, as a negative truth. It was supposed to be derogatory, somehow inferring that I was kept from certain outside influences, so I must not be very wise. The older I got, the more this negative sentiment grew surprisingly positive as I became thankful for the sheltering of God through the physical manifestation of Godly parents. Thankfully, we have a constant shelter, we have a consummate refuge, we have a place of unequaled security, and we have a place of unfathomable peace. Our constant, our home, our shelter is God. "He who dwells in the shelter of the most high will rest in the shadow of the almighty. I will say to the Lord, "He is my refuge and my fortress, my God, in whom I trust" (Ps. 91:1–2).

At the beginning of each move, when the boys entered a new school, one question always arose. Who was going to be the non-family contact person? Thankfully, we always have family when we arrive no matter where our destination. We have the family of believers. We have the family of God. In a way, the connectedness we immediately had with other believers in Georgia or Turkey or Albuquerque or Guam or Colorado Springs or Clovis or Illinois or the Middle East or Miami created for us a sense that we could make this new place home, and we would be supported in our endeavors. Traveling the Seven Churches of Revelation in Turkey, we stopped at the city where the church of Philadelphia had been located. Not many Americans visited that part of Turkey, and the church had not been taken care of and excavated like others had been. We were lost and could not find the location of the church, so with a picture of our desired location in hand, we stopped to ask for directions. The car was instantly swarmed by a huge crowd of onlookers wanting to see us. From the crowd, a man on a moped made his way to us, looked at the picture, and signaled that we were to follow him to the place. Just a short time later, we arrived. Thinking the man did this good deed because he wanted money, Greg offered him some Turkish lira. The gentleman refused, put his hand on his heart, and shook his head. The stranger took out a business card, wrote something on the back, gave it to Greg, and quickly took off before we could see the inscription. On the back of the card he had drawn the sign of the fish, an ancient and continuing secret sign of a believer within a culture that disallows Christianity. This Turkish man, a stranger in a Muslim country, was our brother. The security of God feels like home, and His people gathered together feels like home.

We are currently planning for our forever home. I'm not talking about heaven, which Ben as a child described as "infinity strawberries". I am referring to our retirement home, which we in the military often call our forever home. As a military family, we were always just "passing through," never planting roots for long. In the same way, God is currently preparing our eternal home. "In my Father's house are many rooms: if it were not so, I would have told you. I am going there to prepare a place for you. And if I go and prepare a place for you, I will come back and take you to be with me that you also may be where I am" (John 14:2–3). Well, we aren't preparing a house like God, but we are preparing for our final retirement house. We have been accumulating a list of desires that will be in our future home. We picture a house on a lake in South Carolina where Greg has a workshop, and I have an art and scrapbooking room. We have a fire pit to enjoy on cold nights and a swimming pool to revel in during the hot days. A boat is at the dock ready for use to create memories. The home we picture includes family. "One day when my children are grown I hope they still come through the front door without knocking. I hope they head to the kitchen for a snack, and slump on the couch to watch TV. I hope they come in and feel the weight of adulthood leave them for they are home" (Internet, author unknown). "He who fears the Lord has a secure fortress and for his children it will be a refuge" (Prov. 14:26).

The boys had two different golden retriever dogs growing up. Woody was our first dog and then came Buzz. I guess you now know Ben and Matt's favorite movies growing up: Air Bud and Toy Story. While living in Guam for two years, Woody lived with my dad. The quarantine rules at that time were too long to make it viable for us to bring him. My dad absolutely loved having Woody. He always told the boys how much fun Woody was having running around a large property, swimming in the water hole behind the pasture, and hanging out with him. He told them so the boys would not worry about Woody, but instead, they became very concerned that Woody would not want to be their dog anymore. The two years were over, we had a new home in Colorado, so dad put Woody on a plane, and we were now at the airport awaiting his arrival. Nervously waiting to see Woody, the boys continued to fret that Woody wouldn't know them. His kennel arrived. The door was open, and a-doggy-and-two-boy reunion began. "Woody remembered us, and he wants to go home!" they shouted.

When Ben was in elementary school, he was sad every Sunday night. I couldn't figure this out because he liked school, he was doing well, and he had lots of friends. After time, Ben was able to articulate that it wasn't that he didn't want to go to school, but it was that after a fun weekend at home with the family, he was sad for it to end. That's the best definition of home—having a place you love because it is there that you are loved.

The Final Word

My husband opens his mouth and a deep, rich, beautiful sound echoes with each word. He has a radio voice, a preacher voice, and so many assume, a singing voice. I would agree that Greg could sing wonderfully if he would. But one word spoken to an impressionable boy has resulted in a man's thought that he must not have a voice that could sing. As a youth, Greg sang but was abruptly halted when a group of kids maliciously proclaimed that he sounded like a cow. Greg, with his beautiful bass voice never again sang loud enough for anyone else to hear. Those kids so many years ago spoke the final word, and that final word directed a life.

Not so many days ago, my twenty-four-year-old son Matt shared a story from his childhood that neither Greg nor I remembered. The story began a day when Greg was responsible for taking them to school because I was out of town. Matt had said he felt bad that morning but because he had a baseball game that night, he was going to try to go to school so he could play at night. On the way to school, Matt threw up, so Greg turned the car back to home for Matt's day of rest and recuperation. Because Greg was the baseball coach, he packed Matt up that evening and put him in the corner of the dugout to wait out a game that seemed forever to a young boy feeling very bad but who wanted to play. My twenty-four-year old son then said, "On the way home, Dad said that I was a trooper!" As this grown child was recounting the story, he felt the words of his dad again as he said, "That meant I was a soldier. I was tough!" That one word expressed by a dad impacted a son and directed a life.

We told ourselves as kids that "sticks and stones may break our bones but words will never hurt us." But we only told ourselves that so we could absorb the shock that words create in our hearts and minds. Countless preachers, theologians, philosophers, psychologists, and authors have written about the power of the spoken word. Everybody wants their word to be heard, they want their word to be remembered, they want their word to be the last word. When the boys were growing up, we used to play a game of ping-pong with words that went something like this: Son, "I love you." Me, "I love you more." Son, "I love you most." Me, "I loved you first." Son, "I love you to infinity." Me, "I love you to infinity and beyond." Moms and dads always want to have the last word with their children. Even through the arguing back and forth as to whom literally has the final word, it is a reality that we as parents do have the last word. It is the final word because it is the word that lasts the longest in the lives of our children. It is the final word because it is the word that means the most in the lives of our children. It is the final word because it is the word most often molding the lives of our children and their children to come.

Some military friends visited us when we lived in Albuquerque, so the boys slept on the floor to accommodate the other family of four. Greg and I were getting ready for bed when two hysterical boys ran in our room, announcing that a scorpion had bitten them BOTH. The places on their backs were swelling up, and being from South Carolina, I always thought that a scorpion bite was deadly. I joined the hysteria but also began praying. How could this happen to both boys at the same time? Since Greg is calmer with medical issues, he immediately called the hospital to inquire on our next course of action. The nurse asked the color of the scorpion and determined the bite would be more like a bee sting, so we were just to watch the boys and give them Benadryl. I was not satisfied with one opinion, so I asked Greg to call the number of poison control that was on our refrigerator. He obliged. The voice on the other end seemed quite familiar, and after Greg asked his question, the same nurse from the hospital asked, "Didn't you just call the hospital with the same question?" After confessing that his wife made him call a different number, the nurse explained that it was a different number, but her word on the matter was the same. We had been given the final word, which gave us peace.

Valentine's Day rolled around again, and as usual, Greg and I exchanged gifts. One particular year, the boys had had enough of this ritual and questioned the reason behind Valentine's Day and the gifts we exchanged. Haphazardly, I attempted to interpret our actions by explaining that this day is set aside to show the people in your life how much you love them. I obviously did not do a good job with my description because Ben quickly rebutted, "Well, you love me and Matt. Why don't we get presents?" Manipulated or not, from then on, Valentine's Day became a family event. It became a specific day to communicate, with a token, our love for each other.

The most important token of love we imparted to each other in our house was our final word, which was always the same. Even now that the boys are grown, it continues to be the same. Before leaving the house, before going to bed, before hanging up the phone, before ending a text, we always conveyed one final thought before the silence: I LOVE YOU! We didn't come up with this by ourselves. God's final word through Jesus is "I love you!"

Obviously, this book shows that I love my boys. I didn't count how many stories I told about Ben versus how many I told about Matt. They may count. If they were younger, they would most definitely have counted. After all, if I do for the one, I do for the other. I can say the words over and over that make up stories that we tell about the love for our boys, but the most important word I will tell them is that God's love is the final word. "The Word became flesh and made his dwelling among us. We have seen his glory, the glory of the one and only Son, who came from the Father, full of grace and truth" (John 1:14).

Ben was seven years old and I finished praying over him at bedtime. One of the same requests we often offered was, "Please help Ben love God more every day." Ben finally asked, "Why do you always pray that? Mama, I love God all I can. If I love God more, my head would explode." Considering his question, I told him we prayed that over and over because we loved him.

I thought my four-year-old Matt was asleep, so I slipped beside him to speak words into his life. I began to whisper that God loves him and has big plans for his life. I told him how special he was. As

my heart poured out through my words, I was unexpectedly interrupted by a small voice. "Mom, quit talking. You're waking me up."
Our children may not always be willing or ready to hear the words we
share, but just as Jesus keeps telling us of His love for us, we continue
to speak the word of our love and the love of God to our children.

Thankfully, Greg knew the power and life of God's word: "For
the word of God is alive and active. Sharper than any double-edged
sword, it penetrates even to dividing soul and spirit, joints and mar-
row; it judges the thoughts and intents of the heart" (Heb. 4:12).
Thankfully, he continued to be faithful in sharing the word even
when I was asking him to be quiet.

My first semester as a student at Southern Seminary in Louisville,
Kentucky, Greg was finishing his last semester at Charleston Southern
University in Charleston, South Carolina. On October of that first
semester, Greg flew to Louisville and asked me to marry him. Without
hesitation, I said yes! I couldn't wait to come home for Thanksgiving
to show all my friends and family that I was engaged (this was long
before Facebook). When I first arrived home, Greg made one critical
error in judgment. He took me into a furniture store. For a newly
engaged couple excited to start their life together, this seemed to be
a fun activity, and I was all on board with the idea until we entered
the store. Upon crossing the threshold of the store, fear gripped my
whole being as the fun of the engagement converted to the reality
of marriage and to a life with someone I was afraid I didn't know
as well as I should. Needless to say, I didn't create for Greg or for
my family an atmosphere where they were giving many thanks for
having me home. Fear controlled my thoughts, my actions, and my
relationships that week; and I was mean! By the time I was to pack
up and go back to Louisville, Greg was confused about our relationship, and our pending life together was in limbo. I thought I had the
last word when I instructed him not to call me or write me, just let
me go and we would see what would happen. Upon arriving back at
Seminary, my fear turned to depression, but I didn't have the final
word. Greg never called me. He never wrote me love letters or sent
messages by my roommates pleading his case. He did only one thing.
He sent one final word. He hand wrote Bible verses about fear on

notebook paper. Verse after verse came in the mail, but never with a note attached and never with a name signed. Of course, I recognized the handwriting and decided that since Greg had gone to all the trouble to send these verses day after day, the least I could do was to read them. Then I began doing more than that. I made big posters with each individual verse and covered the walls of my apartment. I memorized the verses he had sent, and I meditated on the word he had sent. Then a miracle happened. The word that was sent, the word that was remembered, the word that was final came alive in me. I came home the next semester to be with Greg and to prepare for our wedding. I was never afraid again. We were married thirty-two years ago. The word is powerful, and it is final in our hearts and in our lives. God has the final word. It is His word. He loves us.

Greg tucked Ben in and whispered to our six-year-old son, "I love you." Ben said, "I know that. I remember everything you say in my head. You always say you love me." The final word is important. It's the last word they hear, it's the continuing word they hear, it's the prevailing word they hear. Let that word be, "I love you!"